TO: DAN

I HOPE

FROM THE FARM AS MUCH AS I
ENJOYED WRITING THEM. THANK
YOU FOR THE BOOK SUPPORT.

Fat Dog Farm *aleah* ♡

Tails of Farm Failures

Aleah Wicks

Copyright ©2019 by Aleah Wicks

This book is a memoir. The author has done her best to make it a tale of truth. It reflects the author's present recollections of experiences. Some names and characteristics have been changed and some dialogue has been recreated.

The resources in this book are provided for informational purposes only and should not be used to replace the specialized training and professional judgment of a health care or mental health care professional. Neither the author nor the publisher assumes any responsibility or liability whatsoever on behalf of the consumer or reader of this material. Any perceived slight of any individual or organization is purely unintentional.

Names: Wicks, Aleah, author.
Title: Fat Dog Farm: Tails of Farm Failures: a memoir/Aleah Wicks.

Email: fatdogfarmnc@gmail.com
ISBN: 9781099868443
https://www.facebook.com/aleah.wicks

In honor of Samosa, my furry soul sister. Without you I would not be my very best me. I am eternally grateful. Until our spirits meet again ...

Contents

Prologue
Samosa's View

Hindsight is always 20-20. Don't I wish I knew that then? For me, it was an era of great confusion. I had continual knots in my stomach from many changes and unknown futures. Had a veterinarian diagnosed me at that time, I am certain I would have been prescribed Valium. Without a crystal ball to foresee my future, I felt lost.

I knew he was not doing well. I tried so hard to invoke a smile. I wagged my tail more and was certain to peer directly in his eyes. I howled in joy when he returned home knowing it always made him happy. He and I were best friends for five years. He was my life. Despite all of my efforts, he became more distant and somber. His wife felt it too. Frozen in her own fear, all she knew was to continue on as if life were regular. He was far from usual though.

The day he took his own life was traumatic for us both. I could smell fear everywhere. I wanted to connect with her given our shared loss. She could not bear to view me. In me she saw him. I now understand. She grabbed my collar and dragged me outside. She left me alone in the yard. Thank goodness there was a large shade tree for me to nap under. The space was small and there was little to occupy my attention. The ground was hot throughout the day and dewy each morning. Soon my skin began to itch. I yearned for the comforts inside my home.

After weeks of being alone, I was grateful to see a smiling face. A woman gathered me from the backyard. She knelt in my presence and gave me a friendly pat on the head.

"I am going to help you. You are off to find a whole new life," she said.

Her smile was large, and her presence was joyful. It was a welcome relief.

She continued to speak as she led me from the backyard into the house and out the front door. I could hear her mumblings but was not paying attention. I was taking in his smell, observing my life again. Little did I know that I would never return to this place.

Her car smelled intensely of flowers. It was overwhelming. I was grateful when she rolled the window down so I could take in the odors from outside. She drove us to a new location, a large building. There were many scents from numerous dogs. There were few windows and aisles of cages. Within each space was a dog I did not know and was not able to formally meet. The days and nights were monotonous. The continual barking from the others drove me mad. I received little comfort or relief in the brief walks and minimal episodes outdoors. This life was lonely too. So, when a small child stood in front of my cage, I knew what to do. Between my experiences these last few days or the giggling overly excited kid that stood in front of me, the choice was easy. I wagged my tail.

"Let's go, Lacey," I heard the young girl say.

Once again, I was attached to a leash being led to an unknown destination. The little girl touched me often and gave big hugs. She smelled of sugar and loved to put her face into mine. She squeezed me tightly throughout the entire car ride.

We pulled up to a house and I felt lucky. I followed her in. The children were kind and loving, but life was intense. The sounds! I heard beeping toys, cartoons playing on the television, and the high pitched screams of small children. All of the chaotic energy blurred my mind. I mimicked what I witnessed. I paced the hallways and barked frequently.

"Quite Lacey. Lay down Lacey. Stop that Lacey," the woman shouted often.

I could do no right. Each day became more difficult.

I knew something was wrong when I went for a car ride without the children. It seemed like I had just left the cold building when I returned again. I felt sad. I missed my best friend and my life.

I lost track of the days inside the cage, until I saw a man. He was paying extra attention to me. He had kind eyes and a comforting energy. I liked him right away. I could not wait to leave with him on yet another leash.

"Meet Santo Lacey." I now had a dog companion. Santo was an instant friend. He was taller than I and had darker fur. He had the look and presence of a wolf. He was the alpha male to my alpha female self. I followed him everywhere. I was so happy with my new dog and human friend. I was finally able to wag my tail in glee. Life was grand again.

My new home also had two small children. The children were sweet, yet a little too engaging. I preferred my days with Santo in the backyard. He and I chased squirrels and small rabbits. We investigated along the house for geckos and barked at the crows in the trees. We were constantly on the hunt. When the children tried to join in our game of chase I growled. I wanted to be left alone. The boys seemed clueless to my signals. I was scolded.

One day I had enough and nipped at the youngest. He would not stop putting his hands on my face, so I put his hand in my mouth. Everyone in the whole house was angry. I knew I was in trouble. I avoided going inside for as long as I could.

I recognized this feeling from my previous home. They were unhappy with me. I heard my name shouted in frustration. They ignored me more and rarely invited me to join family events, while Santo was always asked to play.

Once again, I went for a car ride without the children. I panted and could not settle. Thank goodness the window was down so I could distract myself with the smells along the highway. The drive was long. When we finally stopped, I was happy to see a friendly face. I remember having met him multiple times. I was most fond of the time he snuck me treats. It was winter, and the family sat around a tree they brought inside from the outdoors. A fire was lit in the room all day. There were packages everywhere and aromas of food filled the house. I sat near the table, staring and smelling a plate of sweetness. I wouldn't budge from the table, hoping someone would feed me a goody. I stared at him as he sauntered from the fireplace toward the table. He grabbed a handful of treats. My mouth began watering as I watched him eat the cookie. Quietly he opened his hand near my mouth and I snatched several sugary delights.

I jumped out of the car and sashayed in his direction. He hugged me, "Let's go, Lacey."

I followed the leash for the fourth time and went into another new vehicle. I was sad to leave my best friend Santo, but I was happy I was not back in that building again. My spirit was content as I sat in the front seat of the car for another long drive.

I did not know it at that moment, but the spot where I got into his car, was THE place. Our place. A catalyst that would ultimately positively impact the three of us.

I say let the new journey begin ... but let's hear the whole story through her tale.

1
Samosa

Glancing past the old barnwood-framed picture of my cats and a small Haku horse pottery figurine on my desk, I checked the time. In the pause, I could feel the furrow in my forehead and the intense grip all fingers had on the black ink pen, almost willing the words to come out faster so my charting would be done. It was

5:05 p.m. and the work week was finally over. My body felt heavy and my head was overwhelmed in thought. I was replaying several patients' intakes in my mind. Had I missed any key symptoms that could have improved their overall health? Did I forget to send home a supplement that could provide daily wellness? I knew the answers. Yet, I left the medical office feeling defeated rather than invigorated this week.

Sitting in my car in the work parking lot, while questioning the relevance of my seven years of higher academics, I exhaled deeply and checked my phone. Given the busyness of the day, I missed the opportunity to reply to a group text of my dear girlfriends who were planning the night out with dinner and a movie. The idea of getting lost in a Hollywood cinematic film was appealing, especially considering the group was going to see a Rom Com, *The Proposal*. Still, I was too tired from the heavy work week to consider a night out, even if Ryan Reynolds was the leading man. Instead, I replied with a request for a rain check, and opted to stay home and curl up on the couch with my three cats and a good book.

Once home, I filtered through the mail, hoping for a Pottery Barn or West Elm catalog to distract me. Instead, I was disappointed to find junk bulk coupons from the fast food chain restaurants that I loathed. After feeding the cats and preparing a plate of cheese and crackers for me, I brewed a mug of chamomile tea and grabbed my book. Lost in time while reading *The Help* by Kathryn Stockett, I was startled from the pages when my phone rang. Glancing at the screen, I could see Scott's name on my caller ID. Had my boyfriend's brother ever called me before?

Suddenly my brain shifted to a mild panic wondering if something could be terribly wrong. I pondered these questions for two rings before answering. From the initial greeting, it was clear Scott was upset. His tone was flat and somber, and as he spoke the hair stood up on the back of my arms. Every cell in my body knew something was wrong before the story became known.

Scott and his wife Aisha had rescued a part Great Pyrenees dog named Lacey eight months ago. Scott fell in love with her on first sight. She was a wonderful addition to his family and a perfect companion dog to their family dog, Santo. Still, there had been complications from the get-go ... her continual barking, her stubbornness and fierce independence, and her complete disregard for Aisha's commands. Now the dog had nipped at the children. Scott adored her, but the line had been drawn. Not sure where to go or who to turn to, he called me. He needed time and space for clarity, knowing a plan would have to be implemented to find her another new home. I offered a safe sanctuary as I was child free. I was the best solution Scott could think of at that time.

Stunned by his call and his question, I knew no other words except, "Of course, I will take her right away."

After such a demanding week in the medical field, my mood was elevated by Scott's request. In talking with him and offering my help, I felt useful. As I hung up the phone, I sensed a knot developing in my throat. Suddenly my favorable emotions shifted to feelings of uneasiness. Gazing into the eyes of my cats, I could see my strained reflection. In truth, I was not ready for another dog. I had lost my beloved pug a year before. My heart was still on heavy lock down.

Remmie had been my first dog really, raising her from puppyhood until her death at the age of twelve. Weighing just two pounds when I first laid eyes on her, I couldn't help but melt in her presence. It was 1998 and a brand of stuffed animal toys called Beanie Babies were all the rage. In our first introduction, she was lying in a light pink basket next to a pug Beanie Baby. There was a big yellow bow tied around the handle that softly draped onto the pugs within the base of the basket. In a quick glance, the toys appeared identical. As the ribbon wiggled, it became obvious only one object was a toy, the other was a real-life pug puppy.

Her eyes were large, round, and bulged in their shape. Her snout was nearly immeasurable as a "smashed-faced" animal. While petting her, you could feel extra skin throughout her entire body. I would often rub her folds through my fingertips in a Zen-like meditative fashion while she laid in my lap. It was hard to take her seriously given her looks. Remmie's personality countered that. Where her appearance made you laugh, her intense glares reminded you that she was a force to be reckoned with. She observed more than she partook in life and had no difficulties expressing her thoughts through the use of her comical face.

Remmie was my sidekick and my best friend through my mid 20's and 30's. Her entry into my life marked my adulthood. She was with me in my first marriage. In fact, she was a surprise gift from my first husband. It was his creativity that placed her in the basket alongside her identical stuffed animal toy. She lived with me in my parent's home for six months before we married. She was with me as I earned my master's degree in Acupuncture. She was by my side after graduation, during the long eighteen-hour drive from my home state of Minnesota to my second home in the state of North Carolina. Five years later, she was my companion during a difficult divorce. Her fur trapped the many tears I shed, and her small tongue frequently licked my cheeks to instill cheer. She was a pivotal part of my laughter and light heartedness during my early thirties and newly found single-hood. Ultimately, she was right by my side in my current life with my boyfriend (and future husband) Andrew.

Her shape predicted her future. From puppyhood on, she resembled an overstuffed football. Like a pro-ball player drilled to never drop it, I held her tightly under my arm during the continual change in my quest of self-discovery. It was not until Remmie's eleventh year that I felt more settled. I adored my work at a world-renowned alternative medical clinic in Asheville, North Carolina. More times than not, I felt inspired and empowered in my skillsets as an acupuncturist. Through it, I met like-minded friends and created a new form of family in my holistic community. Not since elementary school had I felt this happy and comfortable with the person who stared back at me in the mirror.

Adding a new dog could potentially throw a wrench into this. The thought of opening my heart to another furry best friend terrified me. When Remmie passed, I was grief stricken. For months I experienced night sweats and dreadful dreams. I avoided going home knowing her little snorty self was not there to greet me. Behind closed doors, I was sad often, feeling lost without my furry best friend. I knew I was nowhere near ready to grieve and experience heavy and negative emotions around a death of a pet, so I avoided all thoughts of ever wanting another.

An hour after hanging up the phone with Scott, Andrew called from Philadelphia. "Did my brother call you?" He asked sternly. "Is he dropping that dog off?"

"Do not worry, dear. The dog is only going to be here for a week. I told Scott I would contact the Pyrenees rescue group and find her a permanent home right away."

I was calm and confident in my conversation. Andrew and I were both clear that taking her in created more discord than either of us was ready to assume. There was no way she would be in our home for more than a week. Two weeks at the most.

Andrew had recently taken a job requiring a move to Philadelphia. I stayed in our home in Asheville while he was away for an unknown duration. When we met, Andrew managed a bank. Our life was simple in that we both had nine to five jobs. We had little responsibility and lots of free time to enjoy everything from global travels, the theater, and outdoor adventures like hiking and biking. Our life was filled with continual fun and great ease. The months of the calendar passed by and our pattern remained. Two years into our relationship, Andrew came home from work one Friday earlier than usual.

"I quit my job," he shouted as he entered the home. "Like the titanic, the banking industry is going down, and I do not want to be on it when it sinks," he uttered with a giggle and flare of excitement in his voice. "I want to study renewable energies."

I was in the laundry room folding clothes. I was grateful to be hidden around the corner from the foyer as he spoke. I could feel my skin flush in response to my anger. What was he talking about? The banking industry is sinking? No way. What the heck are renewable energies? I panicked inside. Of course, I wanted to support him and honor his choice. Still, I could not help but feel scared and frustrated. How could he just do this? Out of the clear blue and while we were in our 30's!

As an alternative medical practitioner, I was trained to view nature for inspiration and understanding of our human world. Through this philosophy, I picture Andrew as tree energy. He is 6'4 and lean. Like the tall oak trees that surround us in the Blue Ridge Mountains, Andrew, too, has a layer of thick bark and deep roots that allow him to remain firm in all he does and thinks. It requires a strong burst of wind to create movement and change when he is rooted and fixated on something. My fears around finances were not going to change his course of action.

If I had my way, he would have hustled back to the bank, tail between his legs, begging for his job back that Friday afternoon. Not because he wanted to work there or that it made him happy. Rather because it was a steady paycheck that made me feel stable. Our life felt known and within it I felt secure. I swallowed my worry, although I could feel it as a lump in the pit of my stomach and ambled around the corner to the foyer wearing my best poker face to give him a hug and announce congratulations.

Andrew enrolled in the Renewable Energies Master Degree Program at Appalachian State in Boone, NC. He was granted onsite housing as a non-traditional student and moved the two plus hours from our home. With Remmie sitting in my lap and my free hand rubbing the looseness of her skin, I cried most of the drive after dropping him off for his first semester. I had little faith in a continued joined life. Still we vowed to remain together, simply living in two different cities over the next few years.

He was close to finishing what would have been his second graduate degree (he already had a Master of Business when we met) when he received a job offer from the largest wind energy utility company in the world. I was smiling ear to ear with him for his accomplishment, honoring his tree-like spirit and commitment to do what his heart yearned for. The pit of worry that sat in my stomach all this time dissolved in this one phone call.

The downside of the offer was that the job was located in Philadelphia. We had been together for over three years, a great portion of our time living in two different cities but connecting during frequent weekends. With this career move, our life would become more complicated. Naturally, challenges would present themselves given that our relationship would continue while living in two different states. We were both aware of even greater unspoken questions: When would our lives combine again? And truly, would they? His job would remain in Philadelphia and I was stubborn and inflexible about moving to the Northeast.

From my first visit to Asheville in 2001, the inner nagging sensation I felt for years to find a place where I belonged disappeared. I could not imagine leaving this city. I was not willing to lose the contentment and happiness I felt while living bathed in the supportive energies and beauty of the Blue Ridge Mountains. Plus, there was no denying Andrew had abruptly quit his job before. Who's to say he would not do it again and Philly would have been all for nothing? Knowing of our inability to find a solution, I knew it was unfair to bring a dog, Scott's huge dog, into our uncertain life.

I stayed in our home in the heart of the city. Our yard was tiny, the size of a postage stamp really. We were crowded by neighbors on all sides. We were on a corner lot situated next to two busy side streets. The home supported the cats. I did not feel it was a good situation for Scott's dog, who was large with an innate drive to roam. The nearly 100-year-old bungalow style house had steep stairs and tiny rooms. Andrew had to duck through the doorways as he entered and exited the bedrooms. The backyard had a four-foot-high wooden perimeter fence and housed my six Silkie hens. Certainly, the dog could jump the short fence and escape. We could not imagine where this dog would fit into this city life.

Scott and Aisha lived in Charlotte. After the initial call, we set a date to meet for the exchange. Inspecting a map, we selected the small town of Landrum, South Carolina to meet as the halfway point the following Saturday morning.

"I want to be there to support Scott," Andrew declared. "I also want to help you the first weekend. She is a big dog and should be on a farm, not live in a city," he hissed.

Andrew made plans to fly home the following week to meet his brother. Although he was highly upset the dog was coming to stay with me, he was equally hurt for his brother. He knew Scott's heart was broken. Animals have been an essential part of Scott's life. Andrew's childhood stories include Kody the family dog, the cat Onyx, and Rupert the bunny, which were all brought into the home from early elementary school, into the college years, thanks to Scott's yearning. Even after Scott had children of his own, Andrew knew the bond Scott shared with his latest pet went deeper than words he could describe. The act of surrendering her was not taken lightly.

I was grateful for his scheduled flight. When I sat in stillness preparing my mind for the upcoming weekend, I could feel an elevated heartrate and warmer body temperature. My mind bogged down in confusion and lacked clarity in how to caretake a big dog. Remmie was a twelve-pound pug with little interest in all things outdoor or "dog-like." Her daily routines required little effort. She woke when I did each day. After a brief moment outdoors, first thing in the morning for bathroom activities, she would saunter back inside for breakfast. As I left for work, she would return to her doggie bed. She spent the bulk of her day sleeping.

The first weekend with Scott's dog was the exact opposite. She was anxious and paced the home continually, barking at all the sounds a city makes. The cars, the horns, and the motor scooters all caused her agitation. To our detriment, her digestive system paid the price of her inner turmoil. Her bowels were loose and frequent, to put it delicately. There were many accidents in the home. Not to mention the smells from her gaseous belly.

Two days later, Andrew flew back to Philadelphia. He was overwhelmed and more determined than ever to rehome her quickly. "You better contact all of our friends who have rescue organization connections," he insisted.

He wanted her gone and he set an ultimatum before flying back. "She needs to be in her new home by the time I return."

With Andrew away, and one less frustrated being in the home, I felt a small sigh of relief. I now had some space to tap into what was going on. Her deep, soulful, and slightly sad eyes reflected her traumatic past. A past that included the suicide of her first owner. After the suicide, she was quickly surrendered to the Humane Society. Her fluffy white coat and big brown eyes were a quick attraction. She invoked images of marshmallows, cumulonimbus clouds, cotton balls, and all things soft. All we wanted to do was snuggle her.

Yet, all of her traumas after the suicide came with her. Her intense behaviors were overwhelming and thus her next home "returned her." Once again at the Humane Society, Scott met her and adopted her as a second family pet and companion to their wolf hybrid dog Santo. Given the nine-month timetable of all these events, it appeared to me that her past confusions, grief, and frustrations came to fruition in our home. As an acupuncturist and holistic practitioner, I wanted to support her. My heart wanted to assist in finding her healing path.

I started with a few acupuncture needles to settle her spirit and used flower essences to ease the burdens on her heart. She greatly enjoyed these treatments. It was not uncommon to find her sleeping in the corner of the house with three acupuncture needles in the top of her head. She always allowed me to rub Star of Bethlehem flower essence on her chest, on her nose, and on the tips of her ears. This flower essence is for those in distress, under conditions such as shock or the loss of someone dear. It is an important remedy to release trauma. Where she was fussy about touch in any grooming technique, she was at ease with all healing sessions.

I allowed her space to process, never reprimanding her indoor bathroom mistakes. I woke multiple times at night to let her outside. During the darkness, she would pace the backyard and bark at the inner-city chaos. I would sit on the side stoop watching her, wishing she would find a place of peace. Through it all, I never found the time nor the motivation to contact our friends with the rescue connections. Without being conscious of it, my heart was opening, and she was wiggling her way in.

Two weeks had passed, and Andrew was still in Philadelphia. It was time to be a responsible pet owner and take her to my local veterinarian. The City of Asheville requires a dog license, and I had not registered her. Furthermore, I needed to name her. She was called

Lacey. It was a name I spoke but strongly disliked. After much contemplation, I called her Samosa. In honor of my favorite cuisine, Samosa was my own personal savory spiced Indian food potato cake.

During the initial examination, the veterinarian was clear. "Samosa is overweight," he scolded. "If you want her to have a long and happy life you need to manage her weight. You need to provide exercise. You need to mentally and physically stimulate her," he commanded.

I was proud of myself for not rolling my eyes during the lecture. I could feel heat in my hands and a warmth flush my face in my agitation. I wanted to tell him she had only been with me for two weeks. That I was an alternative medical practitioner and understood and valued wellness. Instead, I kept my mouth shut. In this pause, I recognized I was triggered. In a society inundated with messages coveted around weight and excessive exercise, I had to check my own imbalance. My fury was with myself and his comments sent me back to the 10-week inpatient treatment center I was admitted to for anorexia when I was 14 years old. I swallowed hard, took a deep breath, and refocused my attention.

He continued instructing, "I need you to stop in every Friday and weigh Samosa on the lobby scale. The receptionist will record her number for me to monitor each week. She needs to lose 15 pounds," he emphasized.

I left the appointment feeling overwhelmed. What else was required to help this dog? Her needs and demands were growing. I was running thin on energy, and lack of restful sleep was not helping. Where would I find the time to create such a vigorous workout plan in order make the "grade" each Friday at our weigh-in? How would I encourage activity in our tiny yard? How would I inspire a dog to play? A dog who was not interested in toys or any amount of the game of fetch. She had one vibe—serious was it. Her 15-pound weight loss goal was daunting. Our weekly weigh-in appointments were weighing on me.

The only solution I came up with was walking and lots of it. We trekked thirty minutes each morning before my workday and nearly an hour each evening when I returned. We covered the City of Asheville strolling by restaurants, passing by hotels, sharing the sidewalks with street musicians and artists. We roamed near parking garages and alongside the many inner-city homes like ours. It was clear through our journeys that Samosa had little socialization. The first time we moseyed near the Haywood Hotel, the automatic sliding glass doors opened. Samosa, closest to the hotel, jumped straight up in the air and twisted her body in a leap toward the street as the lobby doors glided.

Initially, the many city smells caused her olfactory systems to be on overdrive. It was not uncommon to see thick clear saliva hanging three inches on either side of her mouth. The drool persisted for weeks. Yet, at some point, there was a shift. She settled and her barking lessened. She began sleeping through the night and no longer had accidents in the house. It was as if she had a greater understanding of the strange city sounds and smells through first hand exposure. She was gathering knowledge and with it, confidence and empowerment. I too could relax as the sleepless nights became a thing of the past.

We were noticed by many around town. It was hard to miss us. In a sea of small city dogs like Chihuahuas, Maltese, and toy poodles, she appeared like the abominable snowwoman. Car horns would beep, and familiar vocals of friends and clients could be heard shouting in support of our mission. There were no Fitbits then, so I can only imagine the miles and steps we logged each day. We were now some sort of a city mascot. I felt encouraged as it was not just me who was invested in our hikes for her weight loss.

The exercise also released her cooped-up adrenaline. Not only was she losing weight, as witnessed each Friday at our dreaded weigh-in appointments, but she was shedding energetic layers that had been weighing her down too. She barked less. She wiggled her tail more. Her digestive system stabilized. Her eyes appeared lighter and even sparkled some. She nudged the cats, in a playful manner. It was heartwarming to see Samosa begin to find joy again.

When Andrew finally returned for a visit from Philadelphia, he was shocked. The dog he had remembered was no longer in his presence. This new dog was lighter and airy in so many ways. Andrew could see I was smitten with her.

"Well, there is no letting go of her now, is there? We are a city couple with a big farm dog," he muttered with a heavy sigh.

Then, he affectionately touched her head and rubbed her tail as he grabbed the leash for our first family stroll.

Months passed and our routine continued. In friending Samosa, Andrew and I had a new conversation centered around outdoor time and greater space. I yearned for a place where Samosa could run, and I could decrease the intense walking. Farm images came to mind. After all, I was boarding a horse at a stable in Asheville. We now had two farm animals, or wait, consider three if you counted the flock of chickens in the backyard. Even though anyone who has owned Silkie chickens realizes they are more of a designer bird than heritage farm breed.

Farm life supported my love of animals and horses and Andrew's passions of beekeeping, fruit trees, and orchards. Mind you, none of these passions had been acted upon except my recent purchase of a horse. Rather these images were dreams, like sugar plum fairies dancing in our heads. Could we create a sacred space that offered a farm-to-table lifestyle that we enjoyed in the independent restaurant themes of Asheville? Could we find space where Samosa could run free?

As we pondered these questions and images, we researched through Google. The Asheville real estate market was fairly strong in 2011. Our small plot of land and home were all we could afford, so acreage was out of the equation. We expanded our search past the city limits to an area called Tryon.

Tryon was known as 'horse country' and was dominated by equestrian stables. They were big estates with all the picturesque images that come to mind when you think of horse farms: wooden fencing, green rolling pastures, long driveways lined with mature maple trees, and horses galloping in fields. Many of these homes were immediately crossed off of our list due to their hefty price tag. Tryon had two options for us. We made an appointment with a real estate agent and drove 45 minutes south to see the properties.

The first farm appeared to be in the middle of nowhere, even for country-life standards. There were large power lines on the property and deep ruts in the fields. The pastures were not of the green grasses I had imagined, but rather, they were fields of red clay with scrub weeds. There were no views of the foothills of the Blue Ridge Mountains. There was however, a beautiful spring fed pond along with a rustic dilapidated barn. Although Andrew was excited for this property, I disliked it from the beginning.

En route to the second farm, we drove on winding back roads. I was confused and clueless as to our location. Once we arrived, we knew immediately this farm had a lot more to offer. There was a wooden perimeter fence and a beautiful barn apartment with a two-stall barn below. Although this property had many challenges, topography being its biggest as the terrain was steep, the six-mile distant view of the rolling hills of South Carolina captivated me. There were periodic glimpses of the Blue Ridge Mountains in several locations at the peak of the property. We could envision the site of our future home on top of the hill. Given the two farm choices, it was a no brainer—this property was our choice.

Smiling from ear to ear as we left the showing, we set the GPS for the trip back to Asheville.

"You realize this is only three miles and one turn from the exact spot I met Scott eight months ago," Andrew stated. "We are right next to the place I picked up Samosa."

It was as if in the exchange weekend, at the local gas station off of the Landrum exit, Samosa planted a seed. Nearly a year later the seed sprouted. Samosa was our catalyst and inspiration to seek a life that we did not know was even possible. Through her, we were awakening to our dreams and finding a new definition of joy. The crystal ball had spoken; we were to shift from being a city family to being a farm family.

2
Fat Dog Farm

If I had used words like settled, predictable, and stable to describe my life, the next few months would prove to be the opposite. Andrew and I were excited for our new dream, but aware of the many variables that needed to fall into place to render the purchase of the farm possible. In order to buy horse property, we needed to sell our current house in Asheville. The inhabitants in our home were a realtor's nightmare. Just how do you sell a nearly 100-year-old bungalow style house that sits on a tiny lot and includes three cats, a farm dog, and six chickens in the backyard? Where does one begin in this scenario?

Sharing the news with our friends would be difficult too. Our friends had become our family. There was great joy in envisioning our new farm life, but there was equal sadness in letting go of all we had become as Asheville people. How would we release our many downtown adventures? There was no way Tryon had a drum-circle each Friday night or authentic tea experiences as witnessed in the many hours spent at Dobra tea house. What about the eclectic mix of so many outdoor music festivals like Downtown After-5 or Shindig on the Green? Plus, how would I replicate our weekly gatherings centered around incredible foods, laughter, and our family-friends in the city? Would I be happy without all this?

I had little time to explore these internal dialogues because on top of it all, we were planning our wedding in Italy. Andrew has a passion for travel. Our last few adventures had been destination weddings in tropical locations. He yearned for a trip to Europe. In the beginning of 2011, we began saving money for our vacation. We set the date for September and started our countdown for the two-week holiday abroad. After six years of dating, we had many conversations about marriage. Marrying in Italy excited us both.

So, in early spring, we decided to add nuptials onto the trip. Simple enough, right? Boy was I wrong. There were tedious amounts of paperwork required to have a valid marriage not only in Italy, but in the United States too. Much of our free time was spent dotting the i's and crossing the t's for the required marriage documentation. The email exchanges with officials abroad were numerous and tedious. There was much to align to be prepared for our arrival in September of 2011.

Despite the many balls we had spinning in the air, and the stressors that accompanied each of them, Samosa seemed to bathe in the glee of her new life. After six months together, she finally began to initiate play. One day while I was slowly stirring ginger root, cardamom, cinnamon, and nutmeg in a pot of chai tea on the stove, Samosa jammed her nose into my leg and then "grunted" three low toned sounds. "What was that?" Andrew noted with a smile and a glimpse of curiosity on his face peering into the kitchen from the dining room.

"I have no idea but it sure is funny," I laughed.

Samosa peered up at me with her soulful big brown eyes and did it again. I believe the giggling encouraged the behavior more. This specific triple grunt activity would reflect the act of her playing until the day she passed.

Samosa was at peace, sharing her backyard with six Silkie chickens. The hens could often be found nestled into her fluffy white fur. Simply mentioning the word "walk" and Samosa would trot to the door for a stroll downtown. With her weight reduced, the veterinarian ceased the required weekly weigh-in appointments. What a relief! She was now able to sample some of the delights that I purchased during our treks. She and I grew very fond of Vegan Chili Cheese fries from Rosetta's kitchen. Plus, she had a favorite local ice cream shop, Ultimate Ice Cream. They offered a pet's free scoop of freshly made, locally sourced ingredient ice cream. There were many days I meandered alternate routes in order to avoid her temper tantrum should we pass by but not stop in for her free delight.

It was 9 a.m. on a Saturday and instead of walking into the city, Samosa and I chose a different path. In the heat of the late summer morning, we headed toward shade, trekking through the historic Grove Park Inn neighborhoods. The big deciduous tree canopies that line the streets and sidewalks allowed for brief interactions with sparkling sun rays illuminating drops of dew. I was mesmerized while looking up at the large evergreen trees in hues of olive, hunter, and deep green with smatterings of smoky blues from the spruce varieties. Many nationally known and historically important architects had worked within these neighbor-hoods, and their visions can be seen throughout the diverse homes with large stone retaining walls and perfectly terraced grounds.

The beautiful stroll rejuvenated me and once home, I finished all email work in record time. "I am up to date with the embassy in Italy and the requirements for our wedding. What do you think about taking a trip to the farm?"

I had a sparkle in my eyes and softness in my face when asking Andrew. Simply thinking of our potential new life brought about feelings of joy and overall relaxation. There was something about the vision of country life that immediately caused my heart and breath rate to slow. It was as if I just received an hour-long massage picturing the fields of green and horses galloping in my dreamed-of future.

"Let's go. Grab Samosa and we will take a day trip to check the place out again."

Andrew had just finished working on the repair list, getting ready for the sale of the Asheville home. With a nearly 100-year-old house, it seemed as if something always needed attention. Today he was pruning shrubs. He was ready to give his hands a break after being in the yard all morning. This would be our second trip to Tryon. We hoped it would provide ultimate clarity on whether we officially move forward with this purchase once and for all. Without real estate agents, we wished for a quiet trip, answering any last-minute questions, and allowing for final action.

Five miles from the farm, Samosa began "chanting" and "talking" from the backseat. Her vocals overpowered the Ray LaMontagne song, "Trouble," that was paying on the radio. She was excited. She stood tall in the car, wiggling her tail and butt as she howled. "She knows exactly where we are. How could she remember this place from our only visit a few weeks ago?"

I was perplexed. Her excitement put smiles on our faces. It had taken months to wash away her anxieties and serious tone. In this moment of joy, we knew her heart was cleansed from the many traumas of her past. It was invigorating to witness. Like a snake that had shed its skin, Samosa no longer fit into the tight casing that was her previous life. She had expanded and grown into this new dog who wagged her tail often and engaged in all. Right now, Samosa felt much freer.

"We're here!" Andrew announced in fun, knowing very well Samosa was clear on our location.

Once on the farm she leaped out of the car and ran into the wide-open fields. Her bark was contagious, and we ran with her, laughing in delight. There were new sounds surrounding us. The wind was rustling the leaves of the trees. There was a host of birds chirping from all around. Plus, we could hear the whinnying of the neighbors' horses in direct reaction to the sight of this new dog they were seeing on the vacant farm next door.

"That settles it. It is obvious from the happiness the three of us feel right now that farm is going to be our new life."

I was relieved sharing my thoughts with Andrew. Every cell in my body felt comfortable during this second visit.

Watching Samosa illuminate in happiness as she explored the space only confirmed our new vision.

The drive home became known as the power hour. We put together an intense plan for the next thirty days. It was going to require all of our attention and diligence. We needed to sell the Asheville house and place a contingency offer on the farm. After six of years of courtship, we were officially tying the knot while on vacation in Italy. It was going to be our version of an elopement, although friends and family knew of the nuptials. Plus, Andrew was scheduled to move back to Asheville. After 18 months of living in Philadelphia, he received confirmation from the corporate office that he could work from home.

"Its official, my love. I am moving back to Asheville!"

When he called to share the news, I was ecstatic. I had been wishing for this ever since he left for Philadelphia in the first place. He was set to move back just one month shy of our Italian holiday.

Despite the master plan, nothing seemed predictable or quite settled to me. I awoke many days with a mild panicky feeling. The only constant in my life was the twice daily walking routine Samosa and I had in town. After all, we had been doing it for a year now. I reinvested in the task. I found relief and comfort in the ritual, washing away some of my jittery feelings. It's funny how a chore that was once annoying and daunting now became my remedy.

After our second visit to the farm, Andrew stayed in Asheville for the entire week. He utilized the time to clear space and prepare for what would turn into his new home office. During the weekend, we had a lunch date with our dear friend, Ranjeev. Andrew and Ranjeev met in graduate school; they were enrolled in the same Master of Business program at Western North Carolina University. Much of their connection is based in analytical conversations centered around technology, global business, and environmental issues. Sometimes my eyes glazed over, lost in their conversations. Despite the depth of the talks, we always laugh. Together we find comedic relief as we process worldly issues.

"We have news to share Ranjeev. We plan to purchase a farm in Tryon." Andrew sat back against his chair and smiled.

He continued sharing our intentions for the future with the farm being the central focus. I always value Ranjeev's practicality, great intellect, and sense of humor. During this luncheon, I was open and ready for an interrogation.

"Aleah, how does one operate a farm?" he asked matter of factly. "Who cares for the horses? Would you commute into Asheville for work each day?"

Ranjeev continued with his questions. They began to evoke confusion and concern. "Andrew, do you want to be a farmer?" He muttered with a greater influx in tone.

The last question was the most poignant of them all. When I met Andrew, he lived with a roommate in a 700 sq ft apartment in Asheville. He had one plant, a cactus. His only responsibility was a 40 hour per week job managing a bank branch. The rest of his time was spent in the great outdoors of the Blue Ridge Mountains. He was an avid cyclist, both on the road and mountain biking. He loved to paddle the French Broad River. Day hikes of six hours or more in the woods of western North Carolina were frequent events for him during the weekends. He had a passion to be outdoors and to be active, but never was an animal involved.

The vision we presented to Ranjeev was a farm homestead. We described a place that supplied foods from fruit trees, nut trees, beehives, a larger chicken flock, and fresh milk. We told him of our plan to have several horses and utilize the private trail system in Tryon to support my new riding hobby. There was nothing but animals surrounding Andrew in the great outdoors of this picture. Furthermore, Andrew's free time would be spent cultivating and caretaking, not adventure seeking. I, too, began to ponder, "Was the farm vision truly his dream? Or, was it simply mine?"

The conversation continued and we all laughed at our naivety. We were clueless in the specifics of Ranjeev's questions. The truth was, we were both city people having no exposure to farm life. Andrew grew up in the suburbs of Cleveland, and I the suburbs of Minneapolis. The closest encounters we had with chickens during our childhood were on television—Foghorn J Leghorn on

Saturday's Looney Tunes cartoon. Farms were the stinky places you passed along the highway while driving on summer family vacations. Mowing the lawn was a two-hour adventure on the weekend. The heaviest piece of equipment used was a leaf blower. It was clear from this luncheon that we were about to jump into the deep end of the pool, without wearing water wings. I hoped we could swim.

The laughter centered around our cluelessness as farmers continued. Our bellies were full, from eating Indian food and drinking lots of chai tea at our favorite restaurant called Mela. In all of our joy, we nearly triggered the buttons to pop on our jeans. "What are you going to call it, twenty chickens and a fat dog?"

Ranjeev's dimples popped and I saw the mischievous sparkle in his eyes. His statement was hilarious and with tears of joy in our eyes, we knew right then that the farm name came to fruition. In the true essence of our initial relationship with Samosa, the farm would forever be called Fat Dog Farm.

Within 24 hours of placing our city house on the market, we had an offer. We assumed this to be a sign, a clear image we were on the right path. Naturally, the paperwork and logistics needed to be completed while we were in Italy. Once again, we became very comfortable with the East Coast/Italian time zones and with sending technical emails aboard. While in Italy, getting married and on our honeymoon, we signed sales and purchase documents and scheduled multiple inspections. We were communicating with a six-hour time difference and through a house currently occupied by our pet sitter. When in Italy, we turned to food for comfort in all of the chaos.

I ate countless pieces of homemade tiramisu. Andrew's guilty pleasure was authentic gelato, enjoying a healthy scoop a day. We were surrounded by images of pastel villas built into the cliffs above the blue waters of the Tyrrhenian Sea. It was obvious, as my clothes fit a little tighter each day, that I was thoroughly enjoying Italian cuisine. I was grateful I wore a tea length wedding gown with an a-line waist as we were married eight days after our arrival in Italy. Once home, the scale spoke the truth.

We returned from Italy the beginning of October. The closing date had been set for my birthday, November 4th. If we needed another sign to feel confident of our decision, we added this to the list. The days passed quickly as we settled into married life while packing up the Asheville house. We sold the house and purchased the farm with the one attorney, during the same appointment. That certainly made things easier.

Luckily, the mountain air was cool and crisp that fall morning. The U-Haul filled with our pets sat in the attorney's parking lot. We quickly signed all documents rushing back to the vehicles to check on the animals. Andrew drove the car filled with all of the electronics. Gripping the new barn apartment keys, I climbed into the cab of the U-Haul. I peered into the cardboard box with hand poked air holes housing the six Silkie chickens, making sure they were as comfortable as possible. I squeezed my fingers through the metal door of the pet carrier to touch the two boy cats. A separate carrier held our female Persian cat, sitting on the bench seat next to me. Samosa, too, joined on the seat. As I started the truck, she nudged me and grunted her three low tones.

"Let's go Samosa. A new adventure awaits!"

Following Andrew's car, I slowly pulled out of the lawyer's parking lot. The sounds and smells occurring in the cab with me during the 45-minute drive were enough to formulate a howl from anyone's mouth. I giggled, witnessing a few undercoat hen feathers floating in the air. The cooing sounds of the chickens, the meowing cats, and the "chanting" vocals of Samosa all helped melt any sadness I was feeling as I watched my beloved city of Asheville slowly disappear in the rearview mirror.

3
The Horses

We had ten days from the time we closed on the farm and our official move in date until the two horses arrived. Prior to the sale, we purchased a second horse, an eight-year-old Quarter horse for Andrew. He was named Captain P Stuart. We liked his name and referred to him as Cappy, for short. He was a little above average height measuring 16 hands. He had a stocky build and a big muscular hind-end, typical of the Quarter horse breed. His mane and tale were black with one white sock on his right rear foot. His overall body coloring was reddish brown, giving him the distinction of being labeled as a Blood Bay.

We purchased Captain as a trail horse for Andrew and as a companion for my paint mare, Dutchess. She was the same height as Captain, but her shape was vastly different. Her legs were long like a supermodel, and her overall body type was thin and lean. Each paint horse has a particular combination of white and another color. Dutchess' markings were evenly balanced, exhibiting a 50-50 mix of white and light reddish brown. I could picture their matching earth tones in the green fields as complementary bookends to my farm vision.

After signing the paperwork and paying the fee, we hired a horse shipper and scheduled the date for Dutchess and Cappy to arrive from Asheville. We had much to accomplish in order to be prepared for them.

The perimeter of the 18-acre property had a wooden fence. It was poorly constructed with many warped boards and shallow posts. After pushing on a few places and feeling some movement of the wood, we determined the fence would hold for now. We simply did not know how long 'now' would last. We knew we needed to create interior fencing. The day after purchasing the farm, we, the two city slickers, set out to install electric fencing. We bought all the right tools in preparation for this task: gloves, posts, wire, post driver, and wire cutters. We also had our trusty farm sidekick. Samosa enjoyed the smells of the farm as well as her new-found independence. She was able to roam leash free, possibly for the first time in her life, but at least since we adopted her.

It was a cool November morning. Andrew and I grabbed our gloves and stepped outside into the fresh country air. The scenery was stunning with trees exhibiting autumn leaves in all of the fall color and glory. This year, due to an extra dry summer, the leaves had deeper red and golden hues. We both paused to take in the view. Andrew smiled at me, "Let's go, Samosa, we have much to do today."

Samosa followed us into the open field. She inspected all of our new tools and wandered with us while we laid the posts into position. Once the clanging sounds began from pounding the posts into the ground, she adventured off on her own. As she sauntered away, I announced with a laugh, "Well there goes our Lassie. So much for her sprinting toward help should this fence project get the best of us my love."

I had always struggled with spacial relationships. Placing me on 18 acres and now asking for relative size was a nearly impossible task. Gazing out the window that morning, it seemed creating more fence line would be a quick project. A mere few hours and we would have secured a two-acre space. Wonderful! I could use the extra time unpacking and settling into a combined space. Andrew and I had lived apart for most of the 18 months he worked in Philadelphia. Not only was the farm going to be an adjustment, but so was meshing two independent beings into one small barn apartment space.

After several hours in the field, I knew I had grossly underestimated this project. My ears were ringing from the loud ping sounds of the metal post clanking against the metal post driver. I was wearing ear protection, but it buffered few of the piercing tones. It was clear why Samosa left us when she did, given the dull headache I was experiencing from the obnoxious sounds. My hands ached from crimping and pulling heavy gauge wire from post to post. My muscles hurt from carrying the equipment, navigating the hilly terrain, and managing the uneven grounds of the fields. We were one day in and I was nervous that we had bitten off more than we could chew.

Thank goodness it was the first week of November with shorter days. "We better call it complete for now, before we lose our light."

From his flat tone, I knew Andrew was as tired as I felt. The fencing project wrapped up around supper-time. Once inside, I searched for a box marked "kitchen," and hoped to find utensils as well as food. Being one mile from downtown Asheville, we had grown accustomed to wandering into the city and choosing dinner options from a multitude of phenomenal independent restaurants. This was not going to be the case in country life. Plus, as the sunset and darkness entered, I could not see one foot in front of my face. We no longer had the population density of city lights. It was pitch black. I wasn't sure I was able to meander to the mailbox safely even carrying a flashlight.

After rummaging, I found peanut butter and tortillas chips. It was a poor excuse for a meal, but it was food and easy to eat. We were too tired to investigate other boxes. Plus, we were way too exhausted to even consider food preparation and cooking in general. It would be an early turn in, night two on the farm. The bedroom was dark. There were zero city sounds. In fact, it was uncomfortably quiet. That is until Samosa began snoring from the corner of the room. My entire body throbbed. I had dull pains in places I didn't know had muscles. Despite all of this, I slept ... hard.

In Asheville, our house was on a corner lot. We had purchased during the summer and I loved living one mile from the epicenter of the city. Most days I would grab my keys and wallet and hustle to town for fun filled adventures. I enjoyed strolling through the avenues and hearing the many street musicians while window shopping the boutiques. It was the first time I had lived so close to city life and two months in, I was enjoying every minute of it. That was until mid-August, the first day of school. That morning we were startled awake. "Am I hearing diesel engines and bus breaks?"

Andrew was groggy, annoyed, and now clearly wide awake. I jumped out of bed to gaze out the window.

"Oh my goodness, Andrew, there are rows of buses at the stop sign. There must be at least 10 of them!" I snarled in disbelief.

He joined me as we gazed upon the many buses stopped at our corner, waiting to turn left or right and proceed on their various school routes. From August until May, each Monday through Friday, these noises of bus brakes and loud diesel engines would be our new alarm clock. Mind you, a much earlier alarm than we preferred to set. It was a source of great agitation, as well as a comical joke. We vowed from that point on to never purchase a home during the summer.

In contrast, the barn apartment was quiet. Samosa even slept late. My eyes naturally opened in a casual manner in response to the morning light. It was nearly 7:30 a.m. Andrew and I peered at each other and simultaneously screeched, "No buses!"

We chuckled and enjoyed our first peaceful morning during a school week as we were now living in Tryon.

The calm start renewed me. I was ready to tackle yet another day of fence work. I was not about to eat a second meal of peanut butter and tortilla chips, however. Thank goodness we had our wonderful Silkie hens. I went outside to the chicken coop and collected four eggs for a quick and delicious breakfast. The food situation was still in disarray as we adjusted from meals away from the home to meals solely on the farm. With a belly full of protein and a mug of hot green tea, I stared out the window and began to see where our two horses would graze. It was going to be a glorious sight. I could hardly wait for their arrival.

Outside of fencing, other components were needed before the horses moved in. Hay, feed, buckets, and tack for Captain appeared immediately on the list. Certainly, other items were required to have a functioning barn, most of which were unknown to me at that time. After all, I boarded my horse in Asheville and paid little attention to the details required to operate a stable. What a mistake. Rummaging through the local feed supply store, it was clear I was in over my head. As with any supermarket, there were many aisles, brands, and products in the store. Not only did I need to decide which to choose from, it seemed as if I had to pick a color pallet too. Buckets, halters, and feed bins came in all shapes, sizes, and colors. As if these selections were not enough, there were numerous advertisements for products deemed necessary for equestrian life.

Overwhelmed, I imposed a few of my questions onto other shoppers. "You need Vetericyn, horses are always injuring themselves," one woman shared in a stern tone.

"You better get a blanket. It's starting to get cold and you will need to clip and cover your horses," another shouted from the back of the aisle after hearing the conversations.

It seemed as if there were 100 choices and 100 different opinions on which was best.

My studies were of Traditional Chinese Medicine. There were multiple classical texts I could refer to in times of need. These books were thousands of years old, and the information was backed by decades and decades of supportive clinical data. It was easy to find clear, concise solutions and remedies to any question I had. With a little research, I could discover the exact herb or acupuncture point to heal any symptom ranging from indigestion to insomnia. In the horse world, there was a book and subsequent varying opinion for every topic. I was confused. Nothing seemed black and white. I left the feed store feeling incompetent. I made multiple purchases for basic horse needs. On my drive home, I hoped my selections wouldn't harm any in our herd.

The week passed and we were are ready as we were ever going to be for our horses with an interior fence line in place and the barn aisle filled with products for daily farm use. Dutchess had been in our life a little over a year. We knew from our time with her that she lacked confidence and preferred a strong leader. Captain's personality was relatively unknown to us. Cappy lived with two huge draft horses, a breed called Shires. They were gentle giants, yet stern in their attitudes of right and wrong behaviors for herd life. They were quick to discipline Captain when he ran too fast into the barn for nightly grain or when he went to drink out of the water bucket ahead of Ben, the alpha leader. Given their size, Cappy had no choice but to obey their commands. We crossed our fingers when we purchased him, hoping he and my mare would be ideal pasture mates. More importantly, we wished that his exposures with the Shires would meld him to be a confident leader in our herd of two.

Dutchess was smitten with Captain from the start. Her approval of him was a huge relief. Cappy seemed to bask in her admiration. He was often seen strutting around the pasture, tail high, head reaching toward the heavens as if he were an Arabian breed of horse. He carried an aura, resembling that of a king. Dutchess nickered to him often and never let him out of her sight. She followed him around the fields with a schoolgirl crush. This was their routine day after day.

Seeing her standing alone in the pasture after I arrived home from a long workday in the medical clinic in Asheville, caused me great concern. In fact, I was panicked. Something must be terribly wrong for her to have left Captain. I jumped out of the car and ran through the pasture. My high heels sank into the ground with each frustrating step. "Captain, Cappy, where are you?" I shouted.

He was nowhere to be found. As I ran through the field, I noticed a portion of the electric fence had collapsed. He must have gotten out. Where does one begin to find an escaped horse?

After a quick google search, all weblinks instructed me to call the police. My hands trembled as I made the call. The phone rang and rang, and it seemed like several minutes had passed. My mind went blank for a moment when the operator finally answered.

"Do you know how I can find my lost gelding?"

In all of my life, I could never have imagined making this call. Speaking these exact words! It felt like a strange dream. To my surprise, the police officer responded, "We have a report of a lost horse being held at a farm off of Red Fox Road. Could this be your horse?"

"It must be Captain," I stated in delight, "The farm you are describing is near me, my neighbor on the north side of the property."

I thanked him profusely and ended the call abruptly to scamper to my neighbors.

I was wide eyed and still had a little tremble in my hands when I arrived at their farm to retrieve Captain. He was cool and calm, grazing in this unknown pasture. He was a little too calm for my liking. I had just been in a state of panic for nearly an hour, shouting in the fields, wearing my medical attire while searching for him. He was casually munching on grass in their pasture right before me as if life were usual. How dare he!

Our neighbors were kind and supportive. They spoke calmly and softly, recognizing that I still had too much adrenaline surging threw my veins. They giggled as I shared my tale of the last hour, reflecting upon their own innocence in their early farm days. That innocence was now long gone having been in the "horse business" for decades. "It's clear to me," Kevin noted, "Captain is smitten with our mare. Hence his escape."

We owned a farm and horses but did not have a truck or a horse trailer. I thought nothing of it until my first purchase at the feed supply store multiple weeks back. When the young clerk walked out to the parking lot with my many items in tow, he looked surprised when I asked him to put the hay bales, buckets, and feed in the back of a mini suv. A 2008 blue RAV4 to be exact. Now, on the march home with Cappy, I was aware of our farm shortcomings yet again. He didn't seem to mind shuffling alongside the road for the ¼ mile trek back to the farm. He pranced in a display of machismo energy that I attributed to him finding another mare.

Unfortunately, this escape to the neighbor's pasture would not be his last. When I stormed to retrieve Captain for the third time in as many months, he was in a stall in their barn. There was a note on the chalkboard that stated Captain was fine. He had spent the bulk of the day with them. He was munching on their hay. "What is wrong with you?" I growled in frustration after seeing him for the first time since leaving for work early that morning. Once again, Cappy and I sauntered along the road back home. My head was hanging low, his head was held high. He was gloating of yet another adventure.

The next day, I returned home to find a box filled with electrical fence items waiting for us on the front stoop. There was a hand drawn note and instructions from our neighbor Kevin. The directions were clear and precise on how to connect everything properly. Deep down I was embarrassed but, I also felt grateful and relieved for the tools as well as for the directions and help. Clearly, we had a problem and Houdini the horse on our hands. I called Andrew to share the news and to inform him we had a new weekend project.

It would be a busy two days, installing the electric fence as well as our visit from my best friend. Gwen drove down from Asheville late Saturday morning for a day of farm fun. Gwen and I met at work in 2007. She was a Registered Nurse and I the Acupuncturist at the alternative medical clinic. Although our interactions were brief in the office, we knew we had great chemistry with a like-minded attitude and much shared laughter. We explored our connection after hours and attended events together on the weekends. We quickly became the best of friends.

Gwen is the most honest and intimate human I know. She is kind and compassionate and rids herself of all filters to say it like it is. We generously invest in each other's lives with the goal of helping one another. We feel the freedom to speak our truths, pointing out each other's blind spots without consequence or losing the friendship. We share in honesty and humility, and comfort one another through our trials and tribulations. Plus, we laugh at ourselves. A lot! When I leave her presence, I always feel better than when I started.

Gwen arrived late morning. Although it was winter on the calendar, the day felt like spring. The sun was shining, and the birds were chirping. There was a gentle breeze, yet it was warm enough to wear only jeans and a T-shirt. The lilacs were in bloom emitting a sweet smell in the air. Andrew and I had been mending the fence together for a few hours, and the last portion of the electric installation was, thankfully, a one-person job. Gwen and I decided to go for a stroll around the farm while Andrew completed the task. Samosa joined in our adventure.

"Here at the farm Samosa is so peaceful," I noted to Gwen. "She thoroughly enjoys her new job of farm guardian and took to its job description like a duck to water. Samosa innately roamed the perimeter of the fence daily, keeping predators at bay. Plus, she barks at hawks in the air, keeping the hens safe. It's really amazing." I shared in delight.

"You have a no-fly zone here on the farm," Gwen hooted. "Thanks to her watch. Samosa is not the only one learning to live on a farm." Gwen smirked with a wink. "You guys really need a reality television show. You should call it Our First Farm." We both roared.

While wandering back and approaching Andrew, we were discussing the many mishaps that would have been caught on film, had we had a television show. He too chimed in and added a few events I had forgotten. Suddenly, Andrew made a "ziiiitttt" sound and had a little shimmy in his body. Gwen and I wailed, "Oh yes, playing it up for the camera by being shocked from the electric fence." I could hardly catch my breath between chuckles to spit the words out.

Only Andrew wasn't playing. He was actually being shocked by the fence in that moment. Afterward, once we knew he was safe, we all roared! Years later the three of us continue to laugh over this story. It marked such a truth in our reality. In our inexperience as farmers, we were truly clueless. We were in over our heads most of the time. There were many tasks that zapped us into proficiency; it was knowledge obtained by having to survive.

Each day we faced unexpected challenges and were reminded that quiet life in the country was not as carefree as we envisioned. Especially when it came to owning horses. We braced for the continued antics of Captain's adventures. He did not simply leave the farm to create chaos. In his younger years, he was mischievous on many levels. His preferred prank was to wait until I had a wheelbarrow full of manure. The minute I placed my attention elsewhere, he would tip the wheelbarrow over. In a quick action, the entire pile would spill on barnyard ground. On these days, I was shoveling the same poop twice!

One night, I was startled awake to a ruckus in the barn. My immediate thought was a raccoon must be in the feed bins. Armed with a broom, so I could shoo the raccoon out, I cautiously approached the barn door. Peering through the upper glass panel, I saw Cappy. He had knocked the fifty-pound grain container over. Did he escape the stall, or did I forget to lock it properly? The only known truth in that hour was I needed to clean up pounds of spilled feed on the barn floor. It would be a long night.

Captain was our rule breaker. Dutchess was a rule follower. She was stoic and controlled, rarely exhibiting antics of playfulness or joy. When she was unhappy, she deliberately swished her tail. As a device of communication, the tail is an expressive 'talking' part and she used it to the fullest when she felt it was necessary, quickly jerking it from side to side in an agitated manner. If we were not aware of our spatial relationship to her hind-end, she may even swat us across the face in her displeasure. These incidences fortunately were rare.

Lacking confidence, she was always at the back of the pack and because of this, her personality went undetected by most. I first met her at a farm in Asheville in July 2010. I had talked about taking riding lessons for many years. Finally, in my mid 30's I acted upon my desire. Searching the ads in a small local paper, I found a barn just ten miles from home. I called the number and signed up for my first adult riding lesson.

During this session, I was given a tour of the barn and all of the horses who lived there. Dutchess was new to the barn. She had been purchased as an eleven-year-old trail horse. However, when the barn owners placed a saddle on her back, it was clear they had been duped.

She bucked continuously. It seemed as if she had zero saddle experience. After that, Dutchess was turned out into a large herd until a training plan could be implemented.

Upon hearing her backstory, it was hard not to connect with her and feel empathy for her apprehensions around humans. It was clear she preferred horses to people. She had a shifty gaze, glancing anywhere but directly in your eyes. Neither soft touch nor treats seemed to soothe her. After a few weekly riding lessons on a school master horse, the owners of the barn were kind by allowing me to work with Dutchess. It was a win-win situation. Dutchess was getting more human contact and minor training. I had a horse to practice my equestrian communication skills when not in a lesson. We both had introductory abilities and could be seen wandering side by side around the arena.

There is a saying in the horse world that states "green plus green equals black and blue." When you take a human who knows little, and a horse without training, you are guaranteed to see lots of black and blue marks. She and I fell into this truth. Many of our accidents were minor. I had numerous rope burns in my hands from when she spooked and bolted to the other end of the arena. I had my foot stomped on more than a time or two. One time I was so fixated in my focus, peering down at the ground while learning to ride, that I followed my gaze and tumbled over her shoulder and fell to earth.

Nearly a year into trail riding, on a Saturday afternoon, Dutchess and I came across deer. Through the rustling of the leaves, I knew a herd was nearby. The images were limited due to the deep undercover of the woods. Dutchess stopped dead in her tracks. She was frozen in the middle of the trail and would not move. Her head was high, her eyes were wide with the whites of her eyeballs showing. Every muscle in her body was tense. I could feel a tremble building inside of her. I thought it would be best to dismount and lead her past the deer, continuing down the trail. Just as I was throwing my leg over her back to get out of the saddle, she spun 180 degrees and took off. In this maneuver, I was launched straight into the air like the lawn dart game I played in my youth. I ultimately landed flat on my back. Stunned and barely able to catch my breath, I struggled to get up. I needed to find Dutchess. After what felt like a few minutes, I forced air into my lungs and movement in my body. Luckily, she stopped a few feet up the trail and was waiting for me. Adrenaline was still pumping through my veins.

I rode the 45 minutes required to get back to the house. There was no other choice. She and I were in the middle of the trail system, without access for a truck and trailer. Once home and in the comforts of my space, I knew I was badly hurt. My core body temperature plummeted, and I could not stop from shivering. I had a dull headache and a very sore butt. All I wanted to do was go to sleep. Samosa insisted on staying by my side and spent the night in the bedroom.

As it turned out, I had many displaced vertebrae, misaligned hips, and a tailbone hairline fracture. During the next month I utilized chiropractic, acupuncture, and massage therapy treatments weekly to aid in my healing. Samosa followed me on all farm chores, not leaving my side during this time. I did not physically feel like myself for well over thirty days.

I did not break any major bones but something in my spirit broke that day. Such a trauma instilled new fear in me and in Dutchess. My innocence as a rider was lost. As a child I dreamed through movies like National Velvet, the Black Stallion, and Sylvester. I yearned for the day I would ride my horse bareback and bridleless at a gallop on the beach. After the trauma, that dream turned into a nightmare. I no longer felt safe in my hobby and passion.

Samosa became my inspiration in my search for emotional wellness. If she could shed all of the traumas of her past and live in joy on the farm, I was confident I could do the same. My goal was set, the dark of the accident would turn to light and be an opportunity for strength. With Samosa as my muse, I sauntered to the barn and gave Dutchess a kiss on her muzzle. It was a month later and we both remained fragile. I was determined to change our expression. "Let the work begin." My body relaxed within the words as I craved a way to release the fear that brewed deep inside me.

4
Nature's View

I love the mountainous terrain of western North Carolina covered in a plethora of plants displaying color all year. In contrast, Minnesota is vibrant green in the summer and solidly white during many of the remaining months. My eyes are excited seeing red berries on the holly bushes in the middle of winter and my nose tickles at the sweet scent of hyacinths in early spring. I bask in joy staring at the many varieties of azaleas illuminating the ground in hues of yellows, reds, pinks, and whites. By summer, color is aplenty in perennial plants, as well as annual flowers potted in containers displayed on southern covered porches.

In all of the landscape ambience, Southerners relish in outdoor life. One cannot help but slow one's pace in an environment that literally demands to smell the roses that bloom everywhere. The joy of outdoor living includes frequent summertime BBQs. While walking around the side gate to enter a backyard, hickory scents invade your being as you see the ribs cooking on the smoker. Collard greens and vinegar-based slaw occupy a huge portion of the picnic table, and glasses of sweet tea or mojitos are in every hand. Most people stand, unconsciously tapping their feet in rhythm to the Appalachian bluegrass music playing in the background. If the group was small, traditions of my upbringing were the hot topics. Even after five years, I was considered new here. During many evenings, it was not uncommon for someone to ask, "You're from Minnesota, aren't you?"

I do not sound like the characters from the movie Fargo. Although in certain groups, I have been known to extend my "o's" especially when saying the word "boat." I have also been caught using the phrases "you betcha" and "uffdah" a time or two in the company of my southern friends.

The comments and questions were in reference to my personality traits from my upbringing. I frequently heard the statement, "You have a strong and stoic Midwestern work ethic." Initially I was surprised by these words, not fully understanding their meaning. Nearly two decades later, though, I have come to appreciate and comprehend my roots.

Ethnically, many Midwesterns are German, English, and Scandinavian. Through our heritage, we are indoctrinated early that we don't express our emotions publicly. The instructions are never given, but rather observed by examples. You smile and show pleasantries no matter where you are or whom you are with. If difficult topics arise, you involve just the key players and talk about the challenges and muddled emotions behind closed doors. Most importantly, a Midwesterner stays dignified! One needs to handle one's business respectfully and then get on with life.

I was perplexed when a client (and now friend) recommended that I work with Bruce Anderson, owner of the company Nature's View, to help with emotional traumas after my fall. Why would I see someone for this? I was physically receiving acupuncture, chiropractic, and massage treatments for recovery. I knew I needed to obey the equestrian commandment and get right back on the horse. This was my plan. Wasn't getting back in the saddle the only remedy I needed to heal emotionally?

Sensing my indifference to her suggestion, Marcia gifted me my first session with Bruce. It was scheduled for two hours at her home, using a horse from her herd. After a month of hearing tales of Bruce's work and the healing ramifications for others because of it, I was excited to meet him. I did not believe, however, that the session would be life altering. I presumed I would befriend another who valued Mind Body Spirit Medicine. With Bruce, healing would have the added bonus of including horses. I thanked Marcia for her generosity. I held back my callousness, sensing that my inner truth lacked a value attachment. After all, I knew I was handling my business, with dignity, thanks to my roots. I needed to smile widely, pretend as if the fall had never happened and simply ride again.

As I meandered into Marcia's barnyard that afternoon, the sun was shining brightly, dampening the keen focus of my eyes. Squinting, I noticed Bruce was wearing what appeared to me as the famous Crocodile Dundee type hat. He had a lasso rope wound into a small circle in one hand and a red handkerchief tied loosely around his neck. I was stunned to discover that he was wearing shorts, a rare sight in the horse world! Most times lower limbs are completely covered for protection, not to mention hiding the ghostly whiteness of legs and feet when compared to the farmers' tan we sport on our faces and arms.

Bruce was a large man not only in his stature, but in his personality. I could feel his presence many feet before my approach. But, within the first few minutes of meeting him, I was at ease. One cannot help but gain confidence just by being near him. He evoked the image of a protective bear. It felt to me as if he was already my right-hand man, having my back at all times. I exhaled quietly and felt my shoulders drop.

After brief introductions and greeting semantics, Bruce asked me to go inside the round pen and wait for further instruction. As I drifted toward the white metal gate, I noticed a strange latch. It was not the typical chain and clip I was used to seeing around horse farms. This latch was complicated and had a lever, a handle, and a holding bracket. Inspecting all of the pieces, I ignored the chaos and began pushing and pulling. I was leaning into it while willing the gate to open. I could hear Bruce's calm deep voice.

"What tools do you need to open the gate?" His voice was unchanged in its pitch. He continued asking questions in a monotone. "How would you know how to open the latch?" Bruce paused after the second question for what felt like a very long minute, and with a grin asked, "Is it not that the latch needs to tell you?"

I found his riddles confusing. Determined to conquer the task, I eventually bullied the gate wide open and stumbled two steps into the pen in the process. Once inside the round pen, I felt proud, nearly strutting like a cocky rooster. Pausing for a moment, I felt sand under my boots and observed that the white metal panels were encircling a space about 50 feet in diameter. My eyes made their way back to Bruce, who was standing outside of the area. I fixated on his smirk and braced my body for what was next.

There were several more exercises over the next hour. I found each request mildly tedious and more than slightly pointless. Yet, I accepted and performed each challenge. Where was the horse? Did I not sign up for equine therapy? Was it not the horse who would do the therapy? Feeling agitated I tried to calm my judgements and just listen. Bruce continued speaking, all the time instructing me and asking me to find my inner voice, my inner space of known truth.

Nearing the end of my session, I saw Marcia leading one of her horses toward the round pen. What a relief. There would finally be some benefit to this equine therapy! As she approached, I spotted her beautiful black Friesian; a breed of horse that resembles that of a light draught. They have long, graceful, arched necks with thick and flowing black manes and tails. Friesians have silky hair on their lower limbs, deliberately left untrimmed, known as "feathers." Very regal in stature, this breed is in most films where royalty and carriages are involved.

I was grateful to sense that his energy, like Bruce's, was big yet calm. I confidently led the horse into the round pen, unhooked the halter, and let him loose. Where the pace had been slow and methodical, the next fifteen minutes would be the opposite. I was instructed to stay put, to remain in the center of the pen. I was to follow Bruce's cues and directions. Suddenly, his commands piled up. My brain could not keep up in this fast pace.

I could hear Bruce say, "Get the horse to move along the outside rail. Get him to move in a clockwise direction. Have him TROT," a loud emphasis on trot.

Mind you, the horse was roaming loose in the round pen when we started. I was not sure how to get him to move without a lead rope. I knew only to pull or drag him along. Bruce's voice was getting bigger and his tone expressed greater authority. Internally I began to panic. My brain was telling me I needed to forge ahead, complete the task correctly, and do it right now. I could feel the sweat build at the nape of my neck and knew I did not wear enough deodorant. The armpits of my shirt were wet, and my feet began to collect heat. I could hear the pounding of my heart ringing in my ears, and my chest thumped.

Before I knew what was happening, Bruce shouted, "STOP!"

Startled, I turned and stared. "Where are you?" Bruce asked me.

With one quick glance, I was surprised to note I was nearly at the shoulder of the horse. I was so close to the horse that I could touch him. I was nowhere near the middle of the round pen. Bruce smiled softly and began to explain. In this moment it was crystal clear. Where else in life had I lost my center? Where else was I trying to solely accomplish the task? Was I so overwhelmed by requests that I was simply doing activities without direction? The riddles were starting to make sense.

I left my experience with Bruce's work feeling intrigued. I had learned so much about myself in two short hours. I craved more and signed up for multiple meetings. Two of the sessions involved round pen work with my mare Dutchess. She too was healing and working to gain confidence after the negative trail experience we had several months ago. The work with Bruce eased some of our joint fear. I began to have a greater understanding of what was required to be a confident yet calm leader in our herd of two.

I was becoming a more grounded person in general. I gazed at the clock less throughout the day, and nearly forgot about time while in the treatment room. I glided around the acupuncture table, being more present and intuiting of my movements and the sounds exhibited within the healing space. I was more aware and more focused when inserting acupuncture needles. I recognized a hurried breath and consciously slowed it when I felt nervous or rushed. I was becoming a much more centered human.

After four sessions with my mare, in my heart I knew I had to challenge myself. I had unresolved anxieties while riding a recently acquired third horse. With my primitive equestrian knowledge, after the riding accident with Dutchess, I decided I needed a trail savvy horse. Dutchess had spooked badly from the fall which unearthed a fear in both of us. It only made sense to purchase a "bomb-proof" horse for me to ride. After searching the want-ads, we found a twelve-year-old gelding named Indi. He was a Tennessee Walker breed and a rare coveted color called a Blue Roan. The silvering effects of his coat, thanks to an intermingling of white hairs, created an overall blueish hue, hence his name Indigo, or Indi for short. He was stunningly beautiful, and superficially, I admit, his coloration was the main attraction for me to purchase him.

On the ground, he was sweet and behaved like a loving labradoodle. Unlike Dutchess, he craved and enjoyed human contact. While riding him, however, he was a quick horse with lots of fire. He had been trained to move out; go go go was the speed he knew. His ambition and athleticism were far superior to my riding skills at that time. This gap in our connection created tension under saddle. I was stiff and rigid. I consciously made multiple dismounts while riding. I would bail out of the saddle anytime I felt Indi run away. Each dismount instilled greater fear. I was becoming increasingly more distrustful and anxious, and questioned riding in general.

Given the stressors I felt while on horseback, more times than not, Bruce, Indi and I worked outside of the round pen. One session in particular rocked me to my core. We were riding down the open road, meandering in and out of wooded trails. Bruce walked alongside Indi and me, asking more questions, revealing more riddles.

Time progressed and I felt Indi's pace quicken. My body automatically stiffened. My brain went into overdrive, recognizing that we were in a wide-open space. Although I could hear Bruce and knew he was giving me instructions, his voice drifted away. It was as if we were on the beach, Bruce standing on the sand while I was being pulled out by the ocean tide. Fear engulfed me. Indi was now on the move. I felt like I was sitting on top of a runaway train. Tears began rolling down my face, and my hands gripped the reins. I was frozen on top of a moving horse. Luckily, Indi moved toward a fence line. He consciously placed himself in the corner where two metal gates met. He had found a wall, a needed block, in order to stop all movement.

Bruce caught up with us and I dismounted. I could not stop the tears from flowing. My body ached in its tightness. Bruce could sense my raw terror. He understood that I felt unsafe. He hugged me and took hold of Indi by grabbing the reins. As we walked back to the barn, he uttered, "You have uncovered one of your darkest truths. You are at your foundation. I need you to repair the many cracks in it."

He reassured me that Indi was my spiritual and emotional partner. That Indi knew to push me to a place that felt like the brink of my mental sanity. Indi also knew to put himself in front of a fence line to shut down all movement. I could hear Bruce's words and rationalize them, but in my heart, I did not feel this truth.

In hindsight, I now understand that like an earthquake, Indi quickly came into my life and stayed for just a brief moment. His main task was to rattle and shake my spirit down to its skeleton. It was my goal and my responsibility to find out what was left standing after such a disaster.

Throughout the next eight months, as I obeyed by doing my homework and deeply explored the cracks in my foundation, I became the Lotus flower I studied in acupuncture school. Its symbolism is rooted in the fact that the lotus flower's journey does not begin in the open air. Its life begins in murky waters. When the time comes for the bud to flower, the lotus pushes past the unpleasantness of the opaque water. This magnificent flower emerges from the dirty and unclean bottom of a pond. The bud moves through the water to open and welcome the sun on its face. Its beauty remains unstained by its path.

After my intense episode on Indi, I knew I needed to explore my illusions about safety and control. I utilized my connections within the alternative medical world to gain greater access into my unconscious mind. Various healing modalities revealed events of my childhood that are atypical for the greater population. Still, they were my known truths and my upbringing, something I never thought to investigate.

During the first fourteen years of my life, specifically after my parents' divorce at the age of five, my home switched often. The suitcase stayed out. I would pack and unpack, keenly aware of my various needs while living in two different environments. With my mother, we had separate bedrooms, family mealtimes, strict bedtimes, evening chores, and above all, the under-standing to keep a tidy house. With my father, I shared a room with a decade younger sister. We lived on a later schedule—European suppertime and delayed turn in. Several televisions played throughout the day and night as background noise in the home. As a type A personality and with the sometimes dubious virtue of people pleasing, I struggled to find peace while in the busyness and relative disorder of my dad's house.

Within each of my parent's remarriages, I gained additional siblings; two stepbrothers and two half-sisters. My extended family also greatly increased as both my stepmother and my stepfather hailed from Catholic households having six siblings. Through the various healing sessions surrounding my childhood analysis, I was beginning to comprehend my obsessions around control. How could childhood roots grow deep in a forever changing environment?

My younger stepbrother passed at the tender age of four-and-a-half years. For the two years prior to his death, my family lived in and out of St. Paul Children's Hospital. Among my classmates, I was the only kid with knowledge of IV's, chemotherapy, bald heads, and skinny bodies as he was in the cancer ward for many stints. I remember feeling uncomfortable within my own body and the awareness of this form of self in general. It seemed unfair that I had long hair, and a full head of hair where they had none. I knew I had a pudgy face and thick tummy. The children around me had scrawny legs and arms and bloated bellies. More times than not, I felt confused and uneasy with these contrasts. When my little brother passed, sadness naturally engulfed my family. I learned that life is unstable and fragile far sooner than my physical years warranted.

Nearly eight months before my stepbrother's death, my mother was diagnosed with a severe autoimmune disease. It was the summer before my ninth birthday when my mother's health began to fail. She spent a year living in and out of hospitals, fighting for her life. This time though, my brother and I remained home. My mother kept us from the medical environment because of her own fears, as well as protecting us given our history with hospitals. There were many episodes where my grandmother moved in to take care of us, while my mother lay in a hospital bed for unknown durations. Although she found medical stability, her diagnosis and subsequent disease would forever remain a focus. The undercurrent of the family dynamics was centered around a mother who might not be alive for my eighteenth birthday.

The peak of my childhood discomfort occurred in my last year of middle school. I was a pudgy pre-teen, favoring muffins and breads to any vegetable. Sugar was my comfort and pop-tarts became a staple in my diet. I was aware of my larger size and with a peeking interest in boys, I turned to our VHS player and began Jane Fonda workout routines. Wearing a unitard and leg warmers, I fully invested in daily exercise. With this came a new sense of power and a display of control. Becoming extreme, I rid myself of all foods that I labeled 'fattening' and doubled my exercise routine. At some point, rationality ceased. Nearly 40 pounds underweight and with thinning hair and little energy to function, my mother now fought for my life.

It was 1988 and eating disorders were uncommon. Anorexia and bulimia were unheard words and doctors knew little in regard to this field. In fact, American singer Karen Carpenter, who had died five years earlier from complications of this disease, was one of the first to shed light on eating disorders. Doctor after doctor told my mother that I was in a teenage phase and she had nothing to worry about. After four months of evaluations and numerous appointments, finally her prayers were answered.

An echocardiogram from yet another family physician yielded dreaded results. My heart was failing, and I was given less than 48 hours to live. The doctor immediately hospitalized me in the psychiatric ward of Methodist Hospital, the only place in the entire state of Minnesota that had a specific unit for diagnosed eating disorders. I spent the next 10 weeks on lockdown. Although my physical health restored in about six months, my knowledge and understanding of my emotional self remained stunted.

Within the exploration of my foundational cracks thanks to Bruce's suggestion, it was clear that subconsciously, I spent decades controlling every step in the construction of what would become my adult safety net. I made sure my grades were stable and that I was in the top of my class from elementary school through earning my graduate degree. I obeyed household rules and followed specific routines around bedtime and study time. I stuck to foods I knew and liked and did not feel comfortable venturing into unknown cuisines. My circle of friends was small. I pursued relationships that I knew I could count on one hundred percent. With the tears flowing uncontrollably, in that moment on top of Indi with Bruce by my side, I felt my house of cards come crashing down.

It was only from two Somatic Experience therapy sessions where I had to address the effects of my trauma while riding Indi, that the lightbulb came on and I found a complete awareness of my emotional being. Peter A. Levine, PhD developed this technique after observing that prey animals, whose lives are routinely threatened in the wild, are able to fully recover by physically releasing the energy they accumulate during their near-death events. Humans, on the other hand, often override these natural ways of regulating their nervous system by harboring feelings of shame, judgment, and fear. Somatic Experience sessions helped me move past the place where I was "stuck" in my past. I was subconsciously controlling everything, which yielded rigidity and created blocked energy. Indi's frantic pace reminded me of my unstable childhood and the lack of control I felt. Like a lightning bolt that hits an old oak tree, I was split wide open in this moment of chaos and terror. The past unreleased emotions of my childhood were now on full display.

Like a glistening spider's web on a dewy morning, my present life with horses was woven and tethered by the patterns of my past. Gathering and understanding all of my experiences meant that it no longer became necessary to suck it up, put on my big girl underwear, and grit my teeth while riding. Rather, I needed to reset my nervous system, which had been thrown off kilter from events long ago.

In my last Somatic Experience meeting, we had a ceremony. Soft ocean waves played in the background as we took our seats at the craft table. I lit a large pink candle that was encircled with crystals—rose quartz, tiger's eye, and labradorite stones. The mystical energies of these gemstones shed light onto my unknown while bathing me in love and positivity. The two therapists and I wrote poems to the little girl I once knew. We made our own ballads, illustrating her greatness. We drew her pictures of my current life to let her know that although nothing made sense, and was dictated by adults, in the end, she is happy and living her dream.

The space was filled with gratitude. This time, gentle tears rolled out of my eyes. I felt a warmth overcome my body and deep compassion fill my heart for the little girl inside me who was just trying to hold everything together; to not lose anything or anyone else.

Toward the end of our gathering, I smudged the candle, hugged them, and thanked them profusely for my new awareness. I skipped twice on my way to the car. The sun was shining,and I felt invigorated.

I sent a text to Bruce. Over a year later and I was ready to see him again; the cracks in the foundation had been patched. In the encore, his riddles continued, "You have to give up control in order to gain control."

This had been shouted during each session of our past and yet again today. For the first time, thanks to all of my healing workout through the last 365 days, it now made sense. I laughed at myself in light of these words at all of my old patterns' madness. Bruce, too, giggled and said, "Where I am used to seeing tears and self-judgements, I now see a lighter and more balanced you!"

My work through the Nature's View paradigm will forever continue. Within Bruce's approach and continued mentoring, while helping my horses, I ultimately helped myself. His techniques pushed me to explore the depths of my heart so I could become the person my soul was meant to be.

Through it all, my spirit had released much of its core fear. My skeleton survived the earthquake. My grip around my illusions of safety had greatly loosened. And, my heart had been fully restored in all its equestrian glory. I thank my many equine mentors for this, Dutchess and Indi in particular. Still, there would be other horse educators in my future, helping me continue in the re-establishment of my nervous system's balanced and natural rhythm. Thanks to my work with Bruce, I now trusted that I could navigate my way through the uncomfortable with limited interference from the past. I was listening to each moment and in doing so, returning to true humanity by living in the world we were designed for - Nature's World.

5
The Mini Scottish Highlands

Since purchasing the farm six months previously, Andrew and I were finally feeling comfortable. We were adapting from our old city life to our new rural roles. Captain stopped his escapades and was staying home in the pasture with Dutchess each day. Samosa turned into a farm guard dog, protecting the hens and cats. The two boy cats were enjoying life, finding their inner hunter selves by killing mice and snakes in and around the barn. We were finally smiling and relaxing in our new country life.

We had stumbled through the first six months, having more moments of incompetence than competence. It is a miracle that the accidents we endured were of minimal consequence. Days passed quickly with my work as an acupuncturist and Andrew's position as a renewable energy developer. Farm chores consumed the remainder of the evenings. We spent our weekends completing bigger tasks like creating a compost site, installing front entrance gates, and securing a second pasture by adding more electric fence.

Easing into the second half of our first year, we found our farm groove. We had a little pep in our step, a mild cockiness in our new comfort zone. Finally, we were in a state of doing, instead of constantly reacting to all the farm chaos. We bandaged fewer wounds and felt more confident with the farm animals we were caretaking.

The farm now had a daily rhythm with functioning systems in place. The horses behaved better with known routines. We turned them out to pasture at 6 a.m. By feeding them grain at 5 p.m., we enticed them back into their stalls. They had plenty of hay to munch on from suppertime until bedtime when we did a night check around 10 p.m. It was our last opportunity to give them enough hay to eat until the early morning hours.

Samosa preferred being let out of the house after our breakfast. In the city, mornings were a rushed event. As soon as the alarm beeped, I would abruptly bound out of bed, snatch the leash for a brisk trek with Samosa, return home to feed her and the cats, and quickly shower. Grabbing a breakfast bar and a coffee was the final task as I left home for my workday at the medical center.

In the country, the day begin with a much calmer start, including a quiet meal around the kitchen table. Thanks to the new breakfast routine, Samosa stayed inside and was the pre-rinse cycle for the dishes prior to them being loaded into the dishwasher. Samosa was food motivated and never missed an opportunity to snack. After her morning treats, she would scratch at the door to be let out for her farm walkabouts. It was not uncommon to see her return to the shade of the cedar tree near the house in the mid-afternoon.

"I found the perfect gadget." Andrew shared with enthusiasm as he handed me a package at the breakfast table that had arrived from Texas the afternoon before. "It is a battery-operated chicken coop door, which will automatically open at daylight and close at dusk. It works thanks to a solar sensor."

I smiled, finding little value in his newly found tool. I stayed inside to clean up after breakfast while he and Samosa headed into ChickenLand to install the new device. Within one day, my opinion had shifted greatly. I no longer had the daunting responsibility of opening the coop door at dawn. With the new gadget, should I choose, I was free to stay in bed a little longer knowing that the birds had been let out thanks to their solar door. It was a relief to know the chickens had maximum grazing time daily, independent of me. Plus, there was no longer a need to sprint to close the coop door at dark, keeping the chickens safe from the numerous nighttime predators like opossums, raccoons, skunks, and owls. I treasured Andrew's new farm gadget!

In our new-found comfort and routine, it seemed to be a great time to expand our homestead. Our ultimate goal was to have a farm that produced as much food as possible. The fruit trees and vegetable gardens were easy to conceptualize. The farm fresh eggs had been in place since our Asheville residency thanks to our Silkie hens. It was time to tackle something more, and the idea of fresh milk quickly sprung to mind.

Years ago, I had fallen in love with a breed of cow called Mini Scottish Highlands. I was introduced to them via a friend's Christmas card—a family photograph taken on their farm. In this picture, four family members were dressed in black. The Blue Ridge Mountains were the grandiose background. Two Bernese Mountain Dogs sat alongside the mother while the teenage daughter cradled a Rhode Island Red hen. The younger son and father were each holding a lead rope. Attached to the ropes were two shaggy haired mini cows. It was a stunning card on so many levels, but it was the shaggy mini cows that caught my full attention.

I had never seen such adorable cows. Reminiscing on this card from years ago triggered an immediate search for the breed. The Mini Scottish Highlands were described as hardy, self-sufficient, and docile, who calved easily, and thrived in any climatic condition. They were famous for their double coats, making them a unique and fun addition to any hobby farm. "Honey," I shouted from my computer, "They can be used as beef cows, but are also excellent milking cows. Bingo!"

Researching and understanding this breed proved easier than finding them. Most of the miniatures were bred in Texas. There was no way we were traveling 1500 miles to pick up cows. My husband was in the renewable energy field and no matter how I spun the facts and my desires for this specific breed, the negative global impact to retrieve them in Texas was too high. I crossed my fingers and toes that they would appear sometime on the east coast in the near future.

In late March, Andrew made plans to travel to Chattanooga to review a commercial solar site. It was a new destination for him and an opportunity for me to investigate surrounding states for the minis. As luck would have it, after searching Craigslist, I found three mini highlands for sale a little over three hours drive from his work site.

"You will never believe what I found!" I was smiling ear to ear when I shared the news.

"How am I going to drive cows back from a business trip?" Andrew was frank, yet his tone seemed intrigued.

Although we lived on a farm, we still did not have a truck and horse trailer. I knew he was renting a car to drive to Chattanooga. "Why not upgrade to a large SUV with a tow hitch?" I questioned.

With one easy phone call, he changed his reservation from a sedan and secured a big SUV. The plan was quickly falling into place. In fact, I was able to barter with one of my clients, giving her several free acupuncture sessions for use of her horse trailer over a few days.

"By the end of the week, we will have hairy cows on the property." I was visualizing Andrew and me in the Christmas card that held my dreams from years ago. Our farm and all of the furry inhabitants were coming to fruition, and at times I had to pinch myself, making certain it was all real. Self-doubt did creep in sometimes, though saying dreams don't come true, you're not a Disney princess, don't believe this.

Three days later Andrew retuned. "You must see these adorable creatures before we let them out into the field," he called pulling into the farm.

I hung up the phone and immediately ran out the front door in joy and anticipation to greet the new beings. When I approached the back swing doors of the horse trailer, I saw three sets of big brown eyes staring back at me. Their necks were extended upward, gaining a better view of the human who was gazing at them. I reached my hand inside the trailer to pet one. Suddenly, a long lavender toned tongue curled around my entire forearm. It was serpent-like in its movement, yet the tongue was tacky in texture, not overly wet or slimy. The hair on the back of my neck stood up and I felt a little grossed out. Still, the cells in my body were jumping for joy in the presence of the cows. I immediately squashed the voice of self-doubt and felt nothing but gratitude for our new adventure.

The tallest of the three minis was 42 inches in height, and the shortest measured 30 inches at the top of the shoulder. They were compact in size, weighing about five hundred pounds. Luckily for us, the three had different shades of hair making it easy to tell them apart. The tallest one, Fiona, was cream colored. Ami had auburn red hair. The smallest of the three had mocha brown hair. In light of her coloration, we called her Moo-ca. They were sweet and comfortable around humans, but their horns were no joke. If the cows turned their heads and we happened to be standing in the wrong place, we received a healthy whack. It felt to me like I had been hit by one of the Louisville slugger bats my brothers and I played with as children. The horns hurt, and thus intimidated me. I was hyper aware of them and avoided contact at all costs.

Strangely the horses were unfazed. In fact, they all integrated easily into one herd. The minis respected Captain as herd leader; that was all that mattered to him. Dutchess was indifferent as long as Captain was comfortable. In such calmness, we were envisioning our first sets of baby Mini Scottish Highlands and the fresh milk that would coincide with the deliveries and motherhood. Fat Dog Farm was soon to become a functioning homestead after all.

The cows were social and enjoyed attention. Each day I would hang out in the pasture, listening to them munch away on the fresh growth of the spring grasses. Their purple tongues would wrap around the stalkier vegetation to grab a bite. I relished the quiet daily space with the cows.

It was midsummer and a little warmer than our typical hot summer weather, so I waited until the cooler temperatures of dusk before visiting. While sitting in the grass, I noticed a small, pink colored sack hanging from the bottom of Fiona's belly. I called Andrew, asking him to bring the herbal antibiotic cream. I was used to this task given how often the horses scraped their skin. Several times each month, one of the horses would have a small open wound after rubbing against tree bark, fence posts, the edge of the barn, etc. It was nearly second nature for me when applying the herbal salve. It was a quick and easy task, taking only a few seconds to complete. The horses never flinched when applying the cream.

Samosa accompanied Andrew and sauntered into the pasture to greet Fiona. Without hesitation, I knelt alongside her. I put the herbal salve on my fingertips and reached under her belly to apply it. Before my brain could register what happened, I was lying flat on my back next to Fiona. I had intense pain in my shoulder and struggled to catch my breath.

"Fiona cow kicked you. Are you ok?" I knew what Andrew was saying as I heard the phrase before. I did not know it was a literal and true description of cow leg movements. I worked to catch my breath and comprehend what had just happened.

I had a large hoof-print bruise on my shoulder to prove the assault. After two days, the dull ache and red tones in my skin continued. I called a local chiropractor, a referral from the equestrian community. Given the accidents many of my clients experienced in the equine sport of riding, I knew he could help me. Sitting in the Zen like atmosphere of his office, I was reminded of how much my body ached. While the spa music played in the background, I gazed through the picture window into the woodland space. I felt a deep throb from head to toe. While sharing the details of the accident to the chiropractor, I could tell he held back a small smile. It was true, that telling the story out loud I, too, could hear the comedy. I laughed when I finished sharing the details and allowed him to follow in suit. He noted this would be the first time in his twenty plus year history as a chiropractor that the chief complaint would be written as "kicked by a mini cow."

I recovered quickly after the treatment and luckily so. It was summer. Mowing is the main task for every farmer. Cutting the farm grass was no longer a quick weekend chore that I had been accustomed to in all of my other homes since my childhood. Mowing 18 acres of steep and uneven terrain took multiple days and lots of patience. One could hear the low hums of small engines in the distance all around on any given day during the summer months. The smells of fresh lawn clippings would often cause the horses to whinny in delight.

The sun was intense, and the humidity was high this particular day in June. My clothes were stained green from all of the grass clippings and I was saturated in sweat. I stepped inside for a glass of water and a big slice of watermelon. I grabbed my phone to check for any messages. I had a missed call and voicemail from a number I did not recognize.

"Hello, this is your neighbor up the road and I believe your three cows are eating grass in my backyard." Yikes! Andrew was out of town. We still did not have a truck and trailer. I panicked. How would I get them home? I knew I had to come up with a cow retrieval plan before returning the neighbor's call.

The cows' favorite snack was horse grain. It was a challenge to only bring the horses in at night, leaving the cows in the pasture. One whiff of the grain and the cows would barge their way into the barn stalls too. Another phrase I am now intimately connected to—"like a bull in a China shop." It would take all of my strategical planning to herd the horses in and leave the cows out each evening. I grabbed a large bucket of horse grain and called him.

I was grateful the neighbor lived just ¼ of a mile up the road. I began my hike carrying the white five-gallon bucket filled with a large scoop of horse grain. Sure enough, as I approached his land, I discovered my three cows in his back yard. They were so close to his house and his back patio that they were nearly peering into his sliding glass window. They were eating the fresh lawn clippings from his recent mowing. Noticing me, they "moooooed" as if to share, "Look at the goodies we found!"

One shake and sniff of the grain bucket and the three cows turned their attention from the grass and began following me. Each time they became distracted by sights and sounds in neighboring places, I simply scooped out more grain to regain their focus. Their purple colored tongues wrapped around my hand to eat the delights. I was now more comfortable with this movement as the cows were inquisitive and enjoyed using their tongues to investigate everything. Since purchasing the mini cows, more often than not my hands and forearms were wrapped with lavender colored cow tongues. The trek home was quicker than I had imagined. Luckily, I had enough grain to lead them back into the pasture.

"The fence is intact," talking with Andrew. "I could not find the escape site."

We were both confused. After processing the mishap, we concluded their escape was a coincidence. After all, we were used to examining for breaks in the fence thanks to

Captain's past indiscretions. I was confident the entire fence line was in proper working order and categorized the misadventure was a one-time event.

Two weeks later, I received another phone call. "Hi Aleah, it's Beverly. I was out walking my dogs when I believe I caught a glimpse of your cows. At least I think they are yours, but if they are, they are pretty far from home." I thanked Beverly.

Andrew's mother was in town, visiting from Charlotte. His sister had traveled from San Diego to experience the farm. "Our neighbor believes the cows escaped," I shared out loud.

We all went to the various windows, peering into the pastures. "I see horses," hoping I would hear someone say they noted cows from another vantage point. The words were not spoken.

The four of us each grabbed a small bucket and filled it with grain. We got into the car to drive the mile down the road before parking on the shoulder so we could hike deeper into the woods. The cows had ventured much further than they had during their first escape. They meandered through various fields and along other fence lines, nearly a mile deep into the countryside. They were several miles away from home.

After an hour, we finally found the cows scavenging in the fields. They peered at us and "moooooed." It was the same greeting I heard during their first outbreak. I understood the "Hey, look what we found!" excitement in their vocals. It took a long time to lead them home. There were more distractions along this path. After a few choice swear words and many giggles along the way, we were gratefully trekking up the last hill and near our driveway. We secured the three cows in the pasture with the horses. Exhausted, we all went into the barn apartment to sit on the couch and elevate our feet.

"Luckily the cows are safe." Andrew continued, "More importantly, thank goodness they did not cause any damage. After all, we would be responsible for any repairs needed."

His tone was flat. The reality of his words hit home. What if they cows had damaged another's car or even a tractor with their horns? The cost to repair a fence would be minimal compared to the potential damage to neighboring farm vehicles.

I needed to find out how these cows had broken out. After following a few rabbit holes deep into an internet search, I found a few blog sites discussing frustrations with this breed and their double haired coat. More times than not, electric shocks never reached their skin. Without consequence, they were thus prone to pushing through electrical wire and escaping. Barbed wire or wooden fencing was the preferred style for these cows.

I would not use barbed wire. It scared me and I feared for my safety as well as that of our horses. I could picture so many injures with barbed wire. We had dreams of having wooden fencing throughout the property, but such fencing costs tens of thousands of dollars and that project was not even close to coming to fruition.

"We need to think preventatively. What if in their next escape they cause major damage, or heaven forbid hurt a someone?"

Andrew was right. After the two incidences, we knew the Mini Scottish Highland cows needed to be re-homed. It was only a matter of time before they pushed through the fence yet again. We were equally concerned not only about financial damage, but potential damage to communal relations as well. We were still new to our agriculture community and working to establish our roots. We did not need a cow mishap to destroy our ability to flourish in our neighborhood.

Andrew's mom had a co-worker in the Charlotte area who wanted to add more cows to their existing herd. They were intrigued and excited when they heard of our Mini Scottish Highland trio. It was the best situation that could possibly come out of selling the animals I adored. They would live in far lusher and grander pastures. Still, I cried the day the cows left. I adored seeing their soulful brown eyes and hearing the mooing sounds throughout each day.

In the East, elephants are revered and symbolize strong role models of connection to a deeper spiritual life. Elephants are viewed as calm leaders, living in herds of intimate community. They are strong willed and unstoppable when set on a path. They have big ears honoring the ideal to listen more than speak. In the five short months we had them, my mini cows had become my personal form of eastern spiritual elephants. Each time I witnessed their slow saunter in the pastures, I would pause to breathe and slow my own pace. The mini cows carried a grounded energy with each step they took. Being in close proximity to their movements, I could always feel a tribal drumbeat vibration through the earth.

Fiona, Ami, and Moo-ca reminded me never to take life for granted, to remain easy going, and to live in the moment. There had been so many times where I ignored the innocent and plain occasions of a day. Yet, it is in these junctures where the wonder and magic of life exists. The phrase "holy cow" has relevance and inspires virtues of gentleness, calmness, and peace. It is within these attributes that my experiences with our three Mini Scottish Highland cows will forever live on.

6
Keema and ChickenLand

Nearly a year had passed since we sold the Mini Scottish Highland cows. There were continual projects and changes around the farm, none of which created discord. We added two additional horses halfway through the second year. One was a rescued mini horse, found abandoned on a farm near the Tennessee border. We were lucky to have met her in her foster home where they had nursed her back to health. They loved her and helped her reintegrate to living within a herd.

She was curious and attentive, although she was apprehensive of human touch. She was thirty-two inches in height and weighed two hundred pounds. She had all the same energy and attitude of a big horse, simply packed into a fun-size. She was stunningly beautiful, sporting a dark chocolate colored coat with thick golden locks. Her mane and tail were long and full, continually flowing in the wind given her quickened pace in all of her activity. She preferred to trot or strut around the pastures. Andrew liked to refer to her as "Mrs. Fabio." Just like the I Can't Believe It's Not Butter commercials of the 1980s, our mini horse enjoyed tossing her head from side to side flaunting her beautiful blonde hair.

I could not bring myself to call her Mrs. Fabio. Just as I had done selecting Samosa's name, I turned to my favorite cuisine for inspiration. Keema is the name used in Indian savory dishes for small amounts, or something minced. A small twist on the spelling and the name also refers to several profound women of Buddhism. Khema is described as remarkably beautiful and of golden skin.

Keema was our sizzling, small piece of a beautifully golden horse.

We adopted Keema in hopes of finding an animal who could protect our chickens. Protect, a term used loosely in this scenario. Rather, we hoped Keema's silhouette appeared as a dog like image from an aerial view, keeping hawks at bay. Given the farm and its acreage, I was greatly increasing my flock size.

In the City of Asheville, we were limited by code to six hens. Here on the farm, I could have an unlimited amount. During year two, I expanded my birds to include heritage breeds like Marans, Americaunas, Barred Rocks, and Rhode Island Reds. With my new flock, we now appeared to have pre-dyed Easter eggs. Each carton held hues of light brown, light blue, light green, white, and dark chocolate brown colored eggs. Andrew was all for the increased flock. "The chickens are the only thing on the farm of value. They actually produce breakfast," he mumbled under a smile to each horse knowing the hay bill was due soon.

City life forbade roosters ... not on the farm though. The added Silkie boys to create balance, a quality I was trained to detect as an acupuncturist, yielded male Yang energy to the plethora of female Yin hens. Plus, I could hatch Silkie chicks. I could not wait to increase the numbers of my favorite bird. The Silkie is an Asian breed of chicken named for its atypically fluffy plumage. In fact, its name is derived from the feathers as they feel like silk. The breed has several other unique qualities like black skin and bones, turquoise blue earlobes, and five toes on each foot (most chickens have four). They are among the most docile of all chickens and are known for their calm and friendly temperaments. I referred to my Silkies as the Muppets of the henhouse.

During the first year on the farm, the chickens roamed freely. At any given point, they could be found in the barn, in the stalls, under our vehicles, and in the pastures. They were more frequently found in the minuscule amounts of landscaping we had around our home. They destroyed the root systems of many shrubs and herbs. Andrew grew tired of navigating the lands of the home-front, making sure not to accidentally step on or kick a bird. More importantly, he would shout each day while leaving the farm, "I do not want to step in chicken poo!" It was time to create a space for our expanding flock.

My dear friend and multiple generation farmer, Roy, used to joke that every farmer had a PHD, an acronym for Post Hole Digger. In the two years on the property, I, too, was very familiar with this tool. Not fond of it, but familiar. With a new farm project in tow, Andrew and I set out to create a safe and sealed space for the ever-expanding chicken flock. In the end, we installed woven wire fencing on half of an acre.

Samosa was by our side during this weekend project. She laid in the shade of the big cedar tree and watched as we dug over fifty holes for the posts and stretched woven wire to encapsulate the space. Although we were exhausted, we found a new burst of energy with the thought of experiencing the space in action. "Let's move the chickens into their new home," Andrew mumbled with a mild amount of enthusiasm.

Samosa watched from afar. Like eyes following the ball in a Ping-Pong match, she watched as Andrew and I zigged and zagged across the farm. She stared upon us as we stumbled over the uneven terrain trying to catch each bird. "Aleah move left. Grab her!" he would say with an air of frustration and sweat pouring down his forehead.

"Andrew she's bolting for the big pasture, nab Wimbley!" I shouted louder than necessary.

"Behind you Andrew. Get her!" I hollered just as I tripped over a mound of dirt, cursing like a sailor over my clumsiness.

Samosa was never startled by all of our yelling. She didn't react to the high pitch sounds emitted from the chickens either. She was unfazed by the fluttering feathers in the air released from the birds during the chase. She did not assist us. It was clear from the look in her eyes, that she was not a herding dog.

"Samosa come help us!" I yelled.

"Samosa get over here!" Andrew hollered.

She never budged. She was smarter than we were, knowing the effort was not worth the end result. In hindsight, we should have waited until dark to gather the hens. At night you can grab any chicken or rooster without issue. As if they are asleep in your hands, chickens are extremely docile in the dark.

As the weeks passed and the chickens were settled and safe in their new space, I was eager to add more Silkies to my brood. A Silkie hen, however, is challenging to find. After many failed searches on local Craigslist sites, I investigated specific websites for Silkie breeders. At that time, the closet was a breeder in South Carolina. She was two-and-a-half hours from the farm. I knew a five hour round trip to pick up fluffy chickens was out of the question. I held onto her information and checked her webpage weekly for available birds.

Several months had passed. Andrew informed me he was planning a bachelor party for his best friend Nick. The guys wanted a weekend getaway on a lake to grill, swim, kayak, and fish. They selected a campsite in South Carolina that included rental cabins. When I googled the location of the rental cabin, I giggled. What a lovely coincidence, as the rental cabin was a mere fifteen minutes from the Silkie farm.

"You are never going to believe this, my love. Your stag party is near a Silkie breeder I have been following on the Internet." I purposefully avoided eye contact while making this statement. "I checked, and she has several hens that would be a great addition to our flock. Do you think you could pick them up on your way home?"

After what felt like an hour long pause to my question, Andrew finally spoke. "Find out her exact location, and I will see if I can make it work." His tone was direct, lacking emotion.

"You are the best. I will organize all details, so you simply drive to the farm and pick up the cargo." I was enthusiastic and optimistic. What I viewed as a gift; Andrew viewed as an annoyance. Yet, he was willing to help in my yearning for more birds and agreed to pick up the Silkies. Two days later, I contacted the breeder and prepaid for three Silkie hens. The breeder and I had a plan in place for a quick exchange, an easy transaction for Andrew and his friends.

Friday morning Andrew woke early, excited and ready for a guys' weekend. As he drove away, while Samosa and I waved goodbye from the front stoop, it was difficult not to notice the overstuffed Toyota hatchback. He had packed the car with outdoor lawn games like corn hole and the gear needed for the weekend including fishing poles. He had four very large coolers filled with steaks, bratwursts, bacon, few vegetables, and a lot of beer. There were numerous bags of groceries, especially chips. I happily noted my hens would have a space in the car at the end of the weekend after the food was ingested. I could hardly wait to meet my new birds.

An hour into his drive and we had a problem. "The chicken breeder called, and she has a family emergency. You need to pick up the hens right away." My voice was quick and high in tone as I was mildly panicked.

"Aleah, what am I going to do with the chickens all weekend?" I knew to say as little as possible. Three grown men could certainly come up with a plan to house the docile birds for three days.

Later that evening, Andrew called to say he had the hens and that they were beautiful. The guys had constructed a temporary cage off of the front porch so the chickens could be be outside during the day. He planned to collect the them at dusk, allowing them to "roost" in the pet carrier indoors where they would be protected all night.

As the days passed, Andrew sent several videos from his phone. The twenty-second clips would highlight the lake and the beautiful panoramic views. I noticed the guys eating and drinking while seated at the picnic table. Upon further inspection, in the background of the clip, I could see three fluffy hens scratching the dirt for bugs. The cooing sounds emitted from the hens was an oddity for a bachelor camping weekend.

With the new hens successfully added to the flock and ChickenLand in full operation, it was time to add greenery. We had come to rely on the expertise of our new Tryon friends, most of whom were second generation farmers. One such person introduced us to a local nursery specializing in native and edible landscaping. Andrew wanted hardy plants that required little attention and no pesticides. He was like a kid at the candy store, nearly skipping down the rows grabbing plants for his cart. Like the videos we had seen of Black

Friday shopping events, his arms moved in a chaotic rhythm collecting all kinds of trees. I watched as green leaves and flowers filled the air. "Aleah, they have hazelnut trees and persimmons," he blurted in delight. "Look! They have paws paws and ginkgo trees, too!"

In the end, we purchased plums, cherries, nectarines, service berries, paw paws, hazelnuts, persimmons, and even a pomegranate tree. Along the outer fence, we planted muscadine grape vines and rosemary bushes. Andrew envisioned a space where the plants would provide food for us and that which we did not eat would fall to the ground for the chickens to consume. Furthermore, as the trees grew, they would provide shade and shelter for the birds and the farm in general.

He educated me saying, "Chicken poop produces wonderful fertilizer, and chicken scratchings aerate the ground." His enthusiasm was infectious. "Chickens consume bugs, minimizing the negative impact pests have on edible landscaping," he continued.

It was a symbiotic relationship—the chickens, the orchards, the nut trees and vines. The new space became a focal feature on the farm and thus needed a name. Many in our new farm community believed our chickens had found their Mecca. They referred to the space as the Disneyland for hens. It would affectionately be called and forever known as ChickenLand.

Keema lived in ChickenLand by day. At night, she was stalled in the barn with the horses. She seemed to enjoy her daily private space and the fescue grass all to herself. At times, she amused herself by putting her muzzle underneath a hen and gently nudging her up in the air. When we witnessed a hovering chicken floating briefly above, we knew Keema was to blame. The Silkies, in all of their fluffiness and clumsiness, fell victim to her game of play most often. Of course, she utilized this behavior to the maximum around feeding time. She loved organic chicken grain and the birds knew to eat quickly when she was in their presence.

Our plan worked. Where we had lost birds to hawks in the past, we were no longer losing birds with Keema in Chickenland. She was a smart mare with a fierce attitude, frequently prancing around her space. She nickered to the rest of the neighborhood, calling out as if she owned the block. Although she was not a huge fan of human touch, she preferred to stand close to you. We made sure to interact with her during the additional projects we completed in ChickenLand. Other horses would spook and bolt in the presence and sounds of the electric drill, the saw, and the leaf blower. She would remain at our side, calm through it all.

Her role on the farm continued for months. It wasn't until the end of the year that we began to notice an agitation. Within a week's time, we found her galloping the interior fence line of ChickenLand. As we watched this for a few days, we saw that no bird was safe. She would charge, oblivious to their presence, nearly squashing a few hens along the way. I knew something had to change.

Glancing through the window one Saturday morning, I noted Keema frantic. Her head tossed from side to side and she was snorting in frustration. I scampered down the stairs. In the sound of the creaking front-door, Keema charged to the gate. Without thought, I ran to the gate and released her to freedom.

She bolted through the ChickenLand gate and ran onto the driveway. She nickered and tossed her blonde mane. She paced the driveway for several minutes. There was no catching her, she made that abundantly clear. She called to the other horses, grunting along their pasture.

Confused and paralyzed in a thought of action, all I knew to do was open the gate to the main horse pasture. She charged full speed ahead, running toward her much larger herd mates. We presumed she was forever to reign as the queen of ChickenLand. In this one episode, she was now head of the horse herd. At 32 inches in height and weighing one thousand pounds less than the big horses, she became their boss mare.

That was her last day in ChickenLand. Although I did not have the same connection with her as I did to the other horses, I knew she was over the role of chicken protector. Like a teenager slamming the door in anger and disgust, her bolt through the gate displayed the same intent. She was an independent being with her own thoughts for her role on Fat Dog Farm.

Each morning as I sipped my coffee, I gazed out the window to enjoy the herd of three and a half horses.

"Another failure," Andrew would say as we watched Keema instill order in the pasture each day. Like the Mini Scottish Highland cows that never produced milk, our initial farm plan for hen protector fell apart. Our chickens were once again vulnerable to predators as Keema graduated from their space.

7
The Kune Kunes

Andrew was beginning to refer to the farm as a money pit on a regular basis. I needed to find a solution that would allow us to file our taxes with farm classification. At this point, three years after purchasing the property, money was only going out. It was time to change that pattern.

While shopping at a new farm feed store in Asheville, I was introduced to a breed of pigs called Kune Kunes. They are domestic pigs, originally found and kept by the Maori people of New Zealand. They are known for their friendliness, docile attitude, and adorable appearance. The Maori people gave them their name, "Kunekune," meaning fat and round. The pigs come in a variety of colors, have long hair and short snouts. Google research stated they "are an excellent addition to any homestead." "Certainly, our farm is included," I thought with a smile.

In the 1970s, Kune Kunes faced near extinction. Wildlife park owners Michael Willis and John Simister gathered a stock of eighteen (all the Kune Kunes they could find) and began a breeding program. According to the 2012 Kune Kunes Breeders Association, there were less than two hundred registered pigs in the United States. I found my new farm project and the potential to yield profits, although all of my research discussed challenges and difficulties with breeding these pigs. Numerous links shared frustrations with low fertility rates given the pigs are often lazy, fat, and docile. I was up for the task. How difficult could it really be? Wasn't there an innate drive in all species to reproduce?

I now had a legit business plan. For the first time, the farm had the potential to earn a paycheck.

"Cheers to us my love! Kune Kunes husbandry is my new job description" I announced with a huge grin and a sparkle in my eye as if we had just found a buried treasured chest. "Luckily, there are two registered breeders within a six-hour drive of the farm."

"This makes sense. If we sell two litters a year, we can file for a farm classification, and minimize our sales tax. Potentially, we can yield a profit in this lifestyle," Andrew muttered far less enthusiastically than I was feeling.

It was late winter, the season that in the southeast yields mild weather and daffodils in bloom while my family in Minnesota is still in deep in snow and cold. My stepfather, Paul, was visiting, helping with excavating projects on the farm. Paul had gifted us with his amazing excavating skills each year, generously completing big tasks since we purchased the property.

That first year, he created an aesthetically beautiful circle driveway. The initial driveway entered the farm in the middle of the property with a sharp angle and steep incline. Paul created a new entrance at the first corner which meandered toward the barn apartment. The new road was much wider and almost completely level. He added a circle, making it easier for trucks and trailers to enter and exit. In this, our third year, Paul tackled a project at the highest peak of our eighteen acres. On the top of the hill, he cleared and leveled the land to make a huge horse-riding arena. This was no easy task, as he had to move tons of dirt to flatten the area for my new space. In all, it took over three weeks to complete.

On a cold and rainy morning in March, I knew working outdoors would be bone-chilling impossible. The arena creation needed to be placed on hold. I had another idea for such a gloomy day.

"Hey, let's go pick up the piglets! Grab the metal dog crate," I spoke in a convincing tone. "Paul, we are taking a road trip," I shouted with a smirk on my face and car keys in my hand.

"I cannot believe we are driving nearly two hours to pick up pigs," Paul declared in a tone of mild disapproval. "I sure hope this cold rainy weather moves out quickly or who knows what other crazy ideas you'll have!"

"No way man. Finally, I have a solid plan," I responded with a wink. "We, and I know you are included, are going to love them!" I could not wait to meet the piglets.

At first glance, Paul and I adored them. Weighing twenty pounds and as wide as they were high, they melted my heart instantly. The baby pigs delighted in our affections and made cute grunting sounds each time we touched them. They were friendly and easily loaded into the crate for the drive home. Peering through the rearview mirror, I was reminded of the trip when we left Asheville for the farm. For that trip, I was surrounded by chickens, cats, and Samosa on the bench seat next to me. Today I was smiling as I peered at two baby piglets in the backseat of the SUV.

Paul chuckled each time the pigs snorted. The giggling continued. It was crystal clear to us that we were smelling hay and listening to pig sounds inside our vehicle while driving through the big city of Charlotte. What polar opposite worlds we were experiencing simultaneously. I noted dander floating in the air as the sun shined through the windshield of the RAV4. The four-lane highway was bumper to bumper with city traffic. This was Paul's first car travel with farm animals and in the congestion, it would take us even longer to arrive home. Watching his eyes express joy mixed with confusion caused my heart to reflect on how far we had come, and how comfortable Andrew and I were as farmers in only three short years.

By the time we arrived back on the farm, the rain had ceased, and the sun began to shine. It was a perfect day to introduce the baby pigs to their new home. Samosa was immediately enthralled. She hovered and constantly sniffed their rear-ends. The piglets enjoyed wandering all over ChickenLand, grunting in delight and nibbling on grass and bits of any residual feed along the way. Samosa shadowed each step they took and followed as they explored their new space. My heart laughed in their presence, and I was in wonder and awe of their species. Their deep brown eyes stared at us with each interaction. They enjoyed our company and would come to us when called. They "talked" often and had an array of vocals to share, their joy, their fear, and their delight, along with basic greetings and semantics. It was also common for them to beg for a belly rub. Being with the Kune Kunes helped me understand why *The Good Good*

Pig, a book by Sy Montgomery that I enjoyed years ago, was written in the first place.

Each Kune Kunes pig has to be registered with the University of California Davis. The program closely monitors breeding in order to promote healthy species and minimize recessive genes. Thanks to the music and inspiration of The Doors, we called our boar Mr. Mojo, and we referred to our operation as The Mojo Rising Line. Given all I had read of the breed, it was clear we needed lots of support to encourage reproduction. Andrew chose the name for the gilt, saying "Priapus is a minor Greek God of fertility and protector of livestock, plants, and gardens. Even though it's a masculine name, it's perfect." We softened it by calling her Pria.

Mr. Mojo and Pria acclimated quickly. They were never bothered by the occasional hen hitching a ride on their backs. Certainly, the chickens enjoyed their very own 'Uber' transport all around ChickenLand, thanks to the accommodating pigs. Mojo and Pria were curious around the horses. Often the herd would lean into the woven wire, with flaring nostrils and displays of snorting in response to what lurked on the other side of the fence. The pigs did not appear to be upset by the unusual sounds emanating from the horses. In truth, the Kune Kunes were the easiest, friendliest, and calmest creatures we had on the farm.

Once word got out that we had this rare breed, many friends and neighbors stopped by. The pigs would entice both children and adults to move in closer with their soft snorting and would dash to the gate to greet anyone who came for a visit. Mojo and Pria would fall onto their sides to expose their tummies, as belly rubs were their very favorite activity. They were more than willing to roll over and enjoy the scratching at any time of the day and with any human. Mild grunting would signal their great delight.

As Mojo and Pria grew, while recognizing our infatuation with them, we continued to present hypothetical financial gain from their breeding. "We could yield more with an additional gilt without too much more work," Andrew declared after crunching the numbers. "We need a second gilt. Let's add a new breeding line."

We selected our next gilt from a successful breeder in Virginia. Once again, on another business trip, Andrew stopped by her farm to pick up our new piglet and then drove her six hours home.

The new piglet was feistier than Pria and differed in appearance. Pria was black and white in color and had markings that mimicked that of a dairy cow. She was also a little taller than preferred breed standards and had a long snout. Her redeeming quality was her large wattles. I find wattles to be bizarre. They are small fleshy tassels that hang beneath the chin and are highly desirable in the Kune Kunes world—the bigger the better. At nearly two inches in length and width, Pria reigned supreme in the wattle category.

Our new gilt was also two toned, a ginger-reddish color with black markings. She had a petite head and short, compact snout. She was much rounder in build than Pria. She was a nearly perfect example of what a purebred Kune Kunes should be. We wanted to name her in continuation with our central theme of love and reproductive support. Andrew and I were married in Ravello, Italy. The picturesque town sat high in the cliffs, overlooking the landscape of Italy's Amalfi coast below. The Old-World gardens of the castle-like Villa Rufolo set the theme for most of the city. Our nuptials in Ravello were romantic, Hollywood classic, and charming. It was a day like no other in our lives together and we wanted to celebrate it. Yes, celebrate in the name of our prized pig we now called Ravella.

Our triplets spent the days foraging and squealing for attention. Mojo was the friendliest of the three. He would greet me each morning with a squeal of hello and an air of good day. He was the first to dash down the hill to meet anyone at the fence line and was always willing to fall at our feet for a belly rub. The more human contact the better, in his world. Pria was a little more aloof and needed to be enticed with a treat for a friendly pat on the head. Ravella was temperamental. She was friendly, but certain to give a high, ear-piercing squeal when she no longer wanted to be petted, or when she demanded more treats.

The pigs were the central focus of the farm and enjoyed all of the glory. They "talked" to the mail lady and the UPS driver each time packages were dropped at the door. They greeted acupuncture clients as they arrived and left the farm. It was not uncommon to behold three snouts smashed up against the gate of ChickenLand anytime someone arrived or even glanced in their direction.

After about three months with the pigs, we noticed Mr. Mojo displaying behaviors of puberty. We presumed it was close to breeding time. With his new interactions, our attentions were focused on him. We spent more time doting on each of the pigs. We began to plan for the girls' labor and delivery. We even sent out "When Pigs Fly—We are Expecting" enthusiastic pregnancy notes. The gestation countdown began; three months and three weeks until the babies were born. The days could not pass quickly enough.

Pria's taller height made it more difficult to detect a baby bump. We were certain with Ravella's stubby little legs and extra-large abdomen that she was pregnant. As I crossed the days off on the calendar, I smiled a little bigger. When the delivery date approached, we kicked the horses out of the barn and moved Ravella into her birthing stall. We prepared her new space by adding extra hay, allowing her to create a nesting spot. She had small buckets with her favorite treats: apples, bok choy, and sweet potatoes. We visited her often, checking for signs of labor or any discomfort.

"I am so excited to meet your babies," I crooned while I rubbed Ravella's belly. "You are going to be an amazing mama."

Thank goodness we lived close in the barn apartment above. I found comfort being in close proximity. After all, this would be our first breeding experience. Andrew and I were childfree. All of the cats and dogs had been sterilized. The horses were gelded. We had only witnessed the hatching of chicks. Partaking in a mammal birth on Fat Dog Farm was going to be a Big Deal. We took turns checking on Ravella in the middle of the night, not wanting to miss a thing. After two days we could not believe she had not gone into labor. Yet, we continued on with our hovering routine.

After four days, Andrew announced, "Something is wrong. We must have miscalculated the conception date." We were confused and disappointed.

Really, we never officially knew the exact impregnating date. Rather we calculated a number based on Mr. Mojo's sexual inclinations. On the fifth day, we moved Ravella from the birthing stall back out to ChickenLand. She protested. She planted her four stubby feet firmly in the barn, squealing when we tugged on her harness.

"Cover your ears, Aleah, I am going to have to push her." Andrew used all of his might to push on her butt, forcing her to move her legs up the hill and join the others. "Man, she is obnoxiously loud," he snarled as sweat formed on his brow line.

Ravella had grown accustomed to the pampering, eating her favorite treats, and experiencing frequent belly rubs. She was upset at being forced to abondon these delights.

The horses were relieved and glad to return to their domain in the barn that fifth evening. It was clear from Captain's response that he was not happy with the pig smells. Cappy, being a bit of a drama king, was very animated. He curled his lip extra tightly that night, exposing his front teeth while inhaling loudly through his nostrils. Typically, he would exhibit this behavior only once—in the presence of an unusual smell. This action often symbolized his dislike. Tonight, he did it repeatedly, and with dramatic flair. It was clear he did not approve of pigs in his barn.

I wish I could say we knew the gestation plan. In truth, we remained puzzled for months. Why weren't they delivering? Were we that far off in our calculations? We continued to watch for labor signs from afar, hoping it would happen any day.

At some point during all of the chaos, the pigs turned one. It was a special day as we celebrated each of their birthdays. The pigs wore festive gold-colored party hats. They were very tolerant of my antics and left the party hats alone. We celebrated by purchasing an organic apple pie from Whole Foods and videoed each birthday event. We never grew tired of re-watching that film. The pigs relished their pie, treating us to extra squeals and grunts of joy. For Pria's birthday, I had even more fun by dressing her in a purple tutu. She looked fabulous.

We were now nearly a year into our connection with the pigs. I adored the Kune Kunes. When Andrew sat me down to process our now failed business adventure, I was distraught. "Something needs to change, my love, as the pigs are costing more money than they are generating. We need to secure pregnancy and fast," he emphasized.

In a panicked state, I returned to Google for deeper research. Low and behold I found pig pheromone sprays available for purchase! For greater success, the company marketed a Boar pheromone spray and Sow pheromone spray. I felt rejuvenated. I had a new tool to add for a successful pregnancy plan. I felt confident we would be back in the farm profit business soon. We spent the fifty dollars and waited one week for the pheromone sprays to arrive.

It was easy to use the product with Mr. Mojo. His snout would wiggle in delight, like the "I dream of Jeannie" character in the hit television show, each time I sprayed him. He had an extra giddy in his step thanks to the boar pheromones. The girls on the other hand, disliked the spray bottle sound as well as the mist that followed. They were quick to jolt out from underneath the liquid. If we were not careful in our actions, the grass received all the pheromones along with Mojo's attention afterward.

Months and months passed, and it was clear we were wrong about everything. The sprays were not working; the pigs were not pregnant. In truth, it became obvious that all three pigs were just really fat. Feeling defeated, we stopped searching for pregnancy signs. We let the pigs live their lives and continued with our regular farm routines.

The Kune Kunes had been on the the farm nearly two years and had not reproduced. They were costing, on average, one hundred thirty dollars each month for organic feed and supplies. Andrew was correct, my business adventure had failed. My dream of farm income through the sale of piglets was unsuccessful. Another farm plan flushed down the toilet.

I justified my failures deciding that since I myself did not have children, how could I lead the pig husbandry project? Knowing first hand how truly special the breed was, I knew it would be easy to re-home the Kune Kunes. I procrastinated in my search for their new home for several months. Despite the dominant pig odors that now dwelled in ChickenLand, and the silly amount of money we were spending to caretake them, I thoroughly enjoyed my relationship with Mojo, Pria, and Ravella. On the day they left for their new home outside of Raleigh, my heart sank heavily into sadness. Like the Mini Scottish Highland cows, not only did I have another failed farm adventure, but I had let these animals down too. I was unable to provide the life I had hoped for all of us.

I shed tears when the mini cows left. I was even more upset losing the Kune Kunes. I would miss Mr. Mojo most. He was quite the character who had a real and constant connection with me and my life. I viewed him as a friend. According to scientific research, pigs know how to learn new skills and thus adapt to complex environmental situations. They are reported as being smarter than dogs. In fact, they rank third in intelligence just after humans and Chimpanzees. It's no wonder I would miss them much, my mini intelligent farm companions.

I received several updates once the pigs moved to their new farm. Their new space gave them larger pastures to roam and other species to provide more entertainment. The new farm raised mini dexter cows as well as Kune Kunes. I found comfort in the updates and was grateful to have found a person who adored the breed as much as I. I continued to miss their presence on the farm and would forever be a fan of pigs, thanks to the two years I was lucky enough to spend getting to know this breed and caretake this intelligent species.

8
The House

Retracing our steps, we lived on the farm over the last four years and it is clear we had more farm failures than successes. One of our farmer friends teased us regularly over our failed endeavors. He would chuckle and say, "Perhaps you should purchase and breed rabbits. If you can't get them to reproduce, we'll have to revoke your farmer badges." It was time we focused on a project that would be successful and not involve animals or a farm business plan.

After losing the Mini Scottish Highlands cows and the Kune Kunes pigs, it seemed wise to stick with two farm species—horses and chickens. Captain, Dutchess, Indi, and Keema lived within our two-stall barn. We created additional space by making an oversized paddock. The paddock was located under a roofed breezeway and connected to the outside stall doors. The design allowed all four horses to stay in contact when they were locked up. At night, one horse was in each stall while the other two remained under the breezeway. The plan worked, although it was not without challenges. Keema would squeal like a pig and kick at the horse next to her if she was left out in a herd of two. She demanded her private stall. Due to our lush grass pastures and thus increased weight, Dutchess had to be placed on a diet. If we kept her in the night paddock, she would steal hay from one of the geldings and eat more calories than warranted. She was truly food motivated, the geldings not so much.

We utilized the easiest plan. Keema and Dutchess had private stalls each night. Captain and Indi stayed in the paddock unless a thunderstorm approached. When the wind picked up and clouds rolled in, Captain would sense the weather pattern change. He would smell the sweet, pungent zing in the air and pace frantically. His eyes would fill with great stress, appearing to bulge out the side of his head mimicking a bullfrog. He would not eat. He would not drink. His anxieties would eventually trickle to the rest of the horses if we did not remedy this quickly.

On stormy nights, Captain settled down within the containment of the four walls. But of course, the change in the usual routine agitated the other horses. We were in a no-win situation during inclement weather. We often woke to rotate the one stall during various intervals throughout the night, although we never displaced boss mare Keema. I came to dread storms with high winds, rain, lighting, and thunder. No matter what time of day, during intense thunderstorms Captain needed to be stalled. It was a tedious and messy process. Most times I would leave the rotation with wet socks, muddy boots, drenched jeans, and a bad attitude.

Selling any of the horses was out of the question. The heartache endured the past four years was taking its toll. Even the death of a chicken, a naturally caused death, could trigger tears and sadness if it happened on an off day for me.

"Andrew, I think we should talk about building a new home and bigger barn," I said seriously after rotating Captain during a thunderstorm. "We already selected the exact home site years back with Samosa." I was rigid in my thoughts and completely over the compact space with the horses.

"The timing just isn't right," he shot back. "Now is not ideal. The farm costs and many failures have created financial stress, and you just quit your job at the medical center," he continued in a monotone.

From the moment we discussed moving to the farm, I envisioned my life continuing in my beloved city. I planned to commute the 45-minute drive daily to Asheville, and assumed I would maintain weekly gatherings with friends, visiting exceptional restaurants and continuing to attend music events, dance groups, and theatrical performances. Surely these parts of my past city life would remain even while living on a farm.

I never believed I could build a full-time acupuncture practice in the very small town of Tryon; I just assumed that I would continue on at the medical clinic. Over the years as we settled on the farm, however, my visits to Asheville dwindled, in part because of the many chores and animal demands. Getting away for six-hour stints generally caused chaos in one realm or the other. Either I was rushing through the morning with rigorous tasks preparing for a day away, or I was working with the animals late as I returned from an exhausting day at the medical center.

Not that we couldn't get away and have fun, of course, but adding an extra hour-and-a-half round trip drive to Asheville to do so created part of the problem. Yet, in truth, no matter how I justified it, I was developing deep friendships and community in Tryon, and it was becoming easier to let go of my old city life. I was enjoying the sights and people where I lived, just in a fifteen-mile radius of the farm. And amazingly, my home acupuncture practice was nearly full. I had not planned on liking Tryon. In fact, I had judged it harshly in the beginning.

"There is no way a sleepy farm town is going to have like-minded people to connect with, Andrew. We'll just continue life as we love it in Asheville," I stated with conviction.

Before moving to the farm, Andrew and I hashed out numerous scenarios; all of the perceived pros and cons of life in the country. I continued sharing my strong opinions that the farm housed the animals, but life would continue in the city.

"We will see my love. I think we are over Asheville," he mumbled with an air of confidence. He knew our life would shift dramatically. He was kind enough to allow me to live in LaLa land for a while.

Samosa could not have agreed more with Andrew. Where I once needed to stimulate her through exercise during our city adventures, I now knew to leave her on the farm. She would turn her nose up, strutting away from any open car door. Farm life was for her. She had a purpose—monitoring the fence line and barking at all of the larger wingspan birds in the skies above. And, she gave me a sense of safety. Andrew's work travels were taking him off of the farm for longer durations. Having Samosa on guard while he was away gave me a sense of peace.

"Let's see if we can swing a loan, my love. If we can secure the funds to build from a bank, it will be a sign!" I suggested as a compromise to move through our stuck conversations.

We were shocked that the local branch of a state credit union would give us a new construction home loan. Prior to their yes, we had received several nos from other major banks. We were now suddenly and surprisingly full steam ahead for phase two of our initial farm dream. A new house and larger barn were in order.

Samosa barked as the construction vehicles entered the farm that first workday. She continued barking and glanced back to me in confusion as the vehicles drove away from the barn apartment, continuing up the hill to the new home site. This would be a daily occurrence for Samosa and a new alarm system for me.

The construction crew and I were challenged through language barriers. My Spanish was poor, and their English did not include vocabulary centered around safety with farm dogs, so I was not sure how to ease their tension during those first few weeks. Samosa's deep baritone bark with snarls, teeth flaring, and growling was pretty intense. She would scare anyone who came to the door unwanted. I'm guessing it was her abundant fluffy white coat that may have eased their initial concerns. That, and the fact that she didn't attack them, especially if they had food. Samosa and the crew were becoming friends.

About two weeks into the project, her barking ceased. I knew the vehicles had entered the farm, and I assumed she was now familiar with the crew and thus did not feel the need to sound the safety alarm. In hindsight, I should have been tipped off earlier. Samosa appeared to be gaining weight, and I had not increased her food or her treats. I thought she was simply growing a thicker undercoat. We made references to her hair growth, that the upcoming winter may be brutal. According to woolly worm folklore, the amount of black on the woolly worm in autumn varies proportionately with the severity of the coming winter. Like the woolly worm tradition, I presumed Samosa's fluffiness was telling us it was going to be a harsh season.

In truth, the upcoming winter had nothing to do with her size. As a food motivated dog, her initial reluctances with the crew dissipated in the bits of breakfast burritos the workers tossed out their car window. Each morning as they drove past her barking near the front gates, a breadcrumb trail, like the one described in the popular Grimm's fairytale, *Hansel and Gretel*, scattered up the driveway. Her svelte figure from the Asheville city exercise routine was long gone. Thank goodness we no longer had weekly weigh-ins at the veterinary clinic. She was the crew's breakfast and lunch companion. She easily added ten pounds in the eight months it took to build the house and barn.

Early on in the building, Paul traveled to the farm to complete another major project. Samosa basked in yet another human who would toss treats and food scraps from time to time. With each yearly visit, Paul grew more comfortable with farm life in general. He reacted less to the crazy antics of the horses, especially while working directly in their pasture. It was not uncommon for me to receive a call saying, "Come collect your horses, they're blocking my equipment again."

Sure enough, I would glance outside and witness the herd standing blandly in front of a piece of his heavy equipment. Most frequently he was halted while in the bobcat as they greatly enjoyed sniffing the ground and rolling in the freshly churned dirt. He found a way to work alongside them, spoiling them with sweets. Paul loved Coca Cola and cans could often be found in the bed of his truck. He also loved the chewy Red Hots candies. The horses would smell the sugar on his lips, and he would secretly let them have samples.

Paul now had his own definition of "Pavlov's Dogs." When his truck was on the farm, it cultivated particular associations between the horses and their sweets. The connections became so strong that he was no longer able to park his truck in the pasture where he was working. If the horses were near his vehicle, they would become hyper focused on treat hunts. Paul witnessed Captain toss a hammer, a level, and other hand tools onto the ground while searching for the sugary snacks in the bed of the truck.

Throughout the construction process, I allowed the horses to graze at the top of the hill. We had not installed a specific pasture there; it was a large space simply defined by the front gates and perimeter fencing. We were waiting until the barn and house were built to ultimately decide where and how big the top pasture would be. On the weekends, while the construction crew was away, I allowed the horses free rein up top.

One particular Saturday, a painting crew made it through our front gates undetected. About an hour had passed before I realized they were working on the house. I suddenly panicked, knowing the horses were roaming freely in the top pasture. I trekked up the driveway to the top of the hill. Getting closer to the construction I could hear familiar sounds. I knew from the past that the horses were rummaging. I braced for a problem.

Reaching the top of the property I saw three men standing in the doorway of the new construction. Their heads were leaning forward, staring in the direction of their vehicle. Their eyes were strained, the brows furrowed, and tension filled their necks and shoulders. In a glance, I noted that their vehicle looked just like Paul's. As they had done time and time before, the horses were searching for hidden goodies in the back of the truck. My mare had tossed two empty five-gallon pails to the ground. The horses were frustrated as revealed in their large and intense movements. This was the truck, but where were the sweets? The horses continued to prance around. The painting crew was worried their vehicle was being mauled right before their eyes.

Quickly, I placed halters on all of them and walked the herd down the driveway into a secured pasture below. "You guys are nothing but trouble," I scolded, even as I laughed out loud.

Although I consider myself to be a practical person, when it comes to living with my equine friends, this adjective seems to slip out the window.

One day while the siding crew was on the farm, I heard a screech from the barn apartment below. Peering out at the pastures, I saw the horses. Samosa was sleeping in the shade of the cedar tree on the island of the circle driveway. I wondered what happened and sprinted up the hill to check on the crew. I was prepared, having 911 ready on speed dial given the pitch of the screech.

Cresting the hill, I spotted Keema's golden locks. She was snorting and prancing about with an air of authority. I giggled inside, seeing nothing threatening in her manner, but rather an actress on Broadway, owning center stage. One crew member ran outside waving his arms above his head and shouting, "Sal de aquí, sal de aquí!" She trotted ahead of him. He was speaking so quickly that I barely made sense of his words.

"A puma was in the house," he babbled out of breath. Wait, what? A puma?

Listening closely, I realized that Keema had sauntered up the front stoop, walked through the front door, and startled the siding crew who were sitting on the floor of the kitchen eating their lunch. Horrified, one man jumped up and chased her out, while another stood with his back against the wall, still believing it was a puma given Keema's size and coloring.

Luckily for us, neither horse incident caused damage to tools or to the building project. Farm mishaps continued, even when we believed there were no more to be had. After all, we were simply building a house, not adding new species to the farm.

It was Thanksgiving time and the house and barn were complete. Samosa was up at least ten pounds, but who was counting. Andrew and I were beyond excited for our new space and the four-stall barn. Restful nights of sleep were ahead for us, no matter what type of weather.

As we stood on our new deck, peacefully gazing at the six-mile distance view and the bulk of our property, we realized it had really been an easy transition. It was seamless to move to the top of the hill from the barn apartment and assume this new space. Perhaps it was because we had witnessed the step by step construction each day during the past eight months. That is how many would explain our smooth transition to the new space.

I believe time is simply to be used as a tool. It has helped me keep order and create space to attend meetings, gather for birthday parties, and be present for work appointments. I know I can put the tool of time away when I am finished with the task. Futures exist through dreams and visions. In this case, Andrew, Samosa, and I had created our home four years previously through a crystal-clear picture as we stood on the top of the hill during the second visit to the farm. Through a wonderous gift I may never fully understand, Samosa planted the seeds of change. Friending and adopting her, just three miles from our future home site, was the initial spark to ignite all our dreams. Now, in a blink of an eye, we had built our forever home and barn. The illusion of time was fast at work. Samosa was our lucky charm.

9
Bodhi

Samosa traveled from the barn apartment up the hill to the new house multiple times each day. It is no small task, trekking up the four hundred feet with a seventy-five-foot vertical climb. It was surprise really, that she had gained so much weight during the construction given the steep incline of our new driveway. Throughout the last year, we noticed Samosa's gait shifting. She was moving slower and with greater attention in each step. She paused at the bottom of the staircase as if she were surveying the task at hand before initiating movement. She slept more each day. It was not uncommon to see her sacked out for hours on end, under the shade of the large cedar tree in the center island.

We weren't sure if it was the steep terrain and additional hiking that caused her extra pain, or perhaps it was her increased weight. Certainly, an extra ten pounds would challenge her joints and overall health. I began having flashbacks to the scolding I received long ago during the first veterinary appointment in Asheville. A part of me began to feel guilty and worry for her increased size.

Then again, perhaps it was not related to her mass as she was almost eleven years old.

The average lifespan of a Great Pyrenees dog is ten to twelve years. Samosa was uncomfortably close to that statistical data. Like the nomadic shepherds who took their sheep into the Pyrenees Mountains bringing along with them their flock-guarding dog, we had become dependent on Samosa's services. Samosa was our brave fortress guard dog, forever immortalized in our logo. The graphic artist who designed our brand years ago was unfamiliar with us. When we hired her over a phone consult, all she knew was we liked earth tone colors and our farm name was Fat Dog Farm. Within two days, she had created the perfect piece. The logo had a silhouette of a dog that was an exact replica of Samosa's outline. It was a wonderful surprise.

Reluctantly, we began searching for a second dog. A huge portion of our hesitation stemmed from being emotionally sad and not wanting to admit Samosa would not be with us forever. We also hesitated because Samosa was a finicky dog with few canine friendships. Like Keema, our mini boss mare, Samosa was a stern leader. She was quick to pounce on the back of any dog she felt was being disrespectful. She equally disciplined any dog she felt was behaving like a spoiled brat. Sometimes she pounced on a dog simply because it was annoying her. More often than not in doggie social situations, we were the ones frantically apologizing as we peeled her off a traumatized and now flipped upside-down submissive pet. Thank goodness she was all sound and fury with no actual damage.

The only dog Samosa fondly interacted with since our move to the farm was my best friend's dog, Flash. Flash was a vizsla mixed breed weighing about forty pounds. He was all muscle and built for speed. When he and Gwen visited the farm, he would sprint circles in the large horse pasture all day long.

Samosa would begin the day by shuffling alongside Flash. That would not last long as she would quickly tire. Suddenly a red blur of a dog would pass by as if it were the month of May with a Run for the Roses in our field. Meanwhile, a white fluffy marshmallow ambled in slow pursuit. Eventually Samosa would stand in the middle of the circle and attempt to dart toward him. She was smart and was shaving off the angles to catch him. Throughout this pursuit, Samosa would grunt, huff, and puff. Meanwhile, Flash continued with his marathon, unaffected with any strain.

We were cautious as we searched for Samosa's companion and successor. The parameters were limited, as the new dog needed to fit the category of guard dog. Sporting dogs and herding dogs presented more challenges on the farm. Their innate drive to chase prey, especially around quick moving and flighty chickens, usually required extra training. We searched the internet for potential rescues in the evenings with Samosa by our sides. Somehow, we had hoped that in her presence she would be able to tell us, "Yes that's it.

Pick that one." We were at a deficit and needed any help we could receive, imaginary or not.

One day, for some unknown reason, I knew to pause over a specific dog. He was a four-year-old Akita-Chow mix. He was labeled as a large dog and appeared to be around Samosa's size from the photos. Although he fell into the guard dog category, we had only heard negative tales of the Chow Chow breed.

"Oh, don't get a chow. They are territorial," one woman declared. "They're terrible with children."

The negative comments continued as we inquired with various friends of their knowledge of the breed. "They need a lot of socialization. You certainly want a puppy, if any, to start them out right. I would not adopt a four-year-old Chow Chow mix!"

Upon researching the Akita, a breed we knew nothing about, we found that they were labeled as challenging as well. They were described as best in a home without children, wary of strangers, and better suited as a one dog household. It was hard to quiet the mind from the lengthy list of challenges presented. Despite all of the negative feedback, something in his photo spoke to me.

He was located with a rescue group in South Carolina. In a week, the rescue would be at a commercial pet food store hosting an adoption event day. I continued with my email communications about the dog and made arrangements to meet him at the adoption event. With

Samosa in tow, off we went for our two-hour drive south.

"Samosa, you need to let us know right away if this is the next farm dog," Andrew announced during our drive.

For the first time in a while, Samosa was enjoying a trip off the farm. She eagerly joined us when we opened the hatchback and invited her along. She jumped right in as if she knew the adventure ahead. We had the windows down so she could take in all of the smells along the way. Her eyes were bright, her tongue was hanging out, and she "talked" throughout the trip.

Seeing him in person, I felt the picture from the internet had oversold him a bit. Disappointment filled me as I gazed upon his scrawny, leggy body. He was not fluffy, nor did he have muscle to counter a puffball build. Unlike Samosa, his eyes were shifty, and he never held a gaze. He was aloof, not connecting with us, not connecting with Samosa. As Andrew walked the dogs in the parking lot side by side, his gait reminded me of a shepherd breed. I was not fond of the slinkiness of his strut. All in all, I was stumped and felt blindsided.

Letting go of my negativity, I did view him as handsome. I loved his reddish-brown coloring. His fluffy gold colored tail that curled up over his back was beautiful and fox-like. His ears were fuzzy, brown in color, and folded over like a teddy bear. The rescue called him Joker, a name that made us both cringe each time we heard it. The group presumed, given our long drive and week-long email interactions, that Joker was going home with us today. In a zombie like fashion, we moved forward with his adoption.

He was unsettled during the car ride home. Samosa clung to the front of the hatchback, avoiding his movement as much as possible. We tried everything to comfort him—encouraging Samosa to interact with him, touching him when in reach, and using soothing vocals to praise him while the slow Muzak-like sounds played on the radio. Eventually we turned the music off and rolled down the windows to draw in the spring breeze. Despite all of our attempts to soothe him, he was anxious. Then he vomited. It was a long and foul-smelling drive home.

"Here is an emotion we know. Ughhhh, I feel defeated again my love." My tone was heavy as we gagged while cleaning up some of the puke at a highway gas station. "I think I am growing more accustomed to failure."

"We need to rename him and change his energy," Andrew declared. "Let's focus on that for the rest of the drive."

Andrew took the lead to clear the heaviness we were all feeling during the stinky ride. His plan worked, as I had something else to focus on. Within a few minutes, I shouted in excitement, "I have it!" Choosing his name came easily. Typically, it took several weeks to rename an animal. It took us four months to rename one of our horses. Learning their personalities was key, as well as noting which tones the animal responded too, before landing on the best fit. The biggest challenge of them all, was for Andrew and me to agree on the new selection. Not this time though.

"Let's call him Bodhi." The name rolled off of my tongue. I continued sharing, "Bodhi is the name of the sacred tree under which Buddha sat and became enlightened. The Buddhist concept of Bodhi is spiritual awakening and freedom from the cycle of life."

"Perfect. What do you think about being called Bodhi?" Andrew was staring into the rear-view mirror at our new dog. "I think he likes it," he voiced with a smile. "Bodhi it is!"

Once home, Bodhi wandered around the property but stayed close to the barn apartment. We considered his afternoon and first day on the farm a success, despite the gross event on the drive. Samosa never snarled at him. She never flipped him on his back in submission. She followed him around as he took in the sights and smells of his new home. They did not dart and play in the pasture as she had with Flash. Yet, we could tell there was an attraction.

Bodhi lived with a family in the suburbs of South Carolina. They had adopted him as a feral puppy, and he had grown much larger than they had hoped. Most of his days were spent in confinement, either in an indoor dog crate or an outdoor run. We would find out later that the initial slinky gait I disliked was directly related to his past crate confinement. He would eventually stand and walk erectly as his Akita breeding warranted.

Bodhi adapted to life on the farm quickly. He never harassed the chickens. He became increasingly more comfortable around the horses, and rapidly learned to leave the cats alone. Initially the cats excited him greatly. Weighing eighty-five pounds, much bigger than Samosa, the cats assumed we had purchased a wolf. They were certain that he was out to eat them. In his company they cowered and cautiously moved from place to place, all the while keeping both eyes locked onto this new creature. Given Bodhi's anxieties and lack of confidence, in the presence of the cats, he displayed little authority.

Despite his positive adaptations and ease on the property, he never took to his farm role with the depth Samosa did. Given the two-hundred-foot descent in terrain from top of the hill to the creekside bottom, he did not monitor fence lines, nor did he gaze to the skies to ward off hawks. He would bark when a vehicle entered the property and then quickly march to the front door. He intensely scratched, frantically wanting inside for his safety and protection. He preferred lazy mornings lounging in the kitchen and evenings on his dog bed watching television. His outdoor adventures were in one-hour stints. Indoor nap-time reigned supreme. Farm guardianship succession was in question.

It was very clear that although Bodhi was a large dog with breeding that supported deep roots of guarding and protecting, he was really a Pomeranian at heart. He and Samosa were the Yin and Yang of each other in our dog world. Where Samosa was independent with great leadership, Bodhi was shy and nearly afraid of his own shadow. Where she would bark and charge, he would cower. Where she would reside outdoors, he would fight for couch space and television time.

Even though they were the odd couple, they enjoyed each other immensely. Each morning they would romp and play outdoors. Samosa enjoyed chasing Bodhi until he would fall on his side. Then she would lightly pounce on his back, biting the scruff of his neck. Before bed they would wrestle between the couch and the coffee table. Again, she would perch on top of him nibbling on his ears. Samosa's eyes were clear and expressive; she loved him. Although we did not understand her pick of him as her successor, we knew for certain of her heart's admiration.

The Chow Chow in Bodhi gave him the appearance of a lion. With a thick, red mane and square and blocky nose and jowl, he appeared to be the King of Beasts. Yet, our dog was more like the Cowardly Lion in the Wizard of Oz. Bodhi's self-esteem was low. It was clear from his behaviors that he believed his fears made him inadequate. He was always last to eat, staying in the rear of the pack, which included being behind the cats. He always verified with us and double checked with Samosa for the final OK before accepting treats. Whenever anyone visited the farm, he was timid and would not approach new people without our guidance and support. We hoped his role as farm guardian would help him gain confidence and change his perceptions.

Bodhi's overall health improved in the first few months as seen through a new lush coat, healthy body weight, and increased muscle mass. The richness and tone of his fur became deeper in hue and had a new sheen. He darkened to the cinnamon red hues the Chow Chow breed is known for. But we noticed a few subtle things with his health that did not sit well with us. From the first walk in the parking lot, it was clear his gait was off. His stance was now more erect, but at times his knees seemed comprised. Sometimes he was hesitant climbing the staircase, and he rarely wanted to hike the steep terrains of our property. He preferred to lie down or sit, standing very little.

Andrew was out of town. I was home cleaning the kitchen after baking homemade biscuits. There was a new local group of women called "Farm Girls." There were monthly classes designed to teach us about farm homesteading, as our great grandmothers would have experienced. There were eight of us in the group. We learned how to hand weave reed baskets, create homemade pie crusts, and make jams. The biscuit-scone class was my favorite. I was baking weekly and enjoying it. If someone had asked me in high school if I saw myself as a farm-homesteader, baking biscuits, I would have snickered in disbelief. Today my belly was laughing in delight from the yummy treats.

I didn't know where the dogs were. My senses were up; it was eerily quiet all around. I glanced through the family room window and noted Bodhi. He was standing still, alone in the front yard. Something was wrong; he was not moving. I immediately ran to his side, hoping to see some motion from him. I knew he needed medical help and that I had to get all eighty-five pounds of him into the cab of the truck. It took all of my might to move and lift him. Of course, it was Sunday late afternoon. I had to drive to the emergency veterinary office in Asheville.

The waiting room was full and busy. There was one continuous bench seat creating a U shape within the space. There were multiple dogs, all weighing less than twenty pounds. There was a French Bulldog sitting on the lap of his human with a large bandage wrapped around his hind leg. There was a Shih Tzu wearing the plastic lampshade cone around his neck. His eyes were sullen. He was sitting next to his owner on the bench seat. There were two trembling Chihuahuas wearing matching pink t-shirts with pink collars and leashes. There was only one dog on the floor, a feisty terrier mixed breed dog that was playing tug of war with his leash and human. All eyes were on me as I slowly and painfully carried my huge lion-like dog into the waiting area. Bodhi cringed as he glanced around the room. He anxiously pawed at my leg wanting me to put him in my lap.

Upon examination, Bodhi's injury was clear. He was lame in his right hind leg. He had torn his anterior cruciate ligament, similar to the ACL in humans which is responsible for stabilizing the knee joint. Bodhi needed immediate surgery. The veterinary office required at least eighty percent of the fee to be paid before they would perform the surgery. Andrew was out of town working on a wind energy project in North Dakota. I knew this was not going to be an easy call.

I was in tears, "Andrew, we have a health emergency. Bodhi needs knee surgery and I am at the medical clinic now. They need to charge our credit card before they perform the surgery."

Andrew was silent for a moment. "What is going on? How much money are we talking about?" His tone was harsh.

The tears continued and I shared the news. "We need to give them twenty-seven hundred dollars." I braced for his response.

Andrew protested. "We are not doing the surgery," he shouted. "Are you kidding me?"

His questions continued as I faded from the conversation. His voice was so loud that those sitting near me could hear him through the phone.

Although my eyesight was blurry from tears, I could imagine the startled glare on the receptionist's face. The wrinkles on her forehead were tense. Her nose crinkled and her lips were held tight. It was obvious she heard Andrew's protest. I was still mildly listening to Andrew argue on the phone when I handed her a credit card for payment.

I knew my husband and his initial reactions in times of financial stress. The receptionist did not. She was very quiet, her facial tension continued. I am certain she was surprised when the credit card charge was approved. I knew Andrew would call back with a change of heart. Worst case, we now had twenty-seven hundred points to use toward a vacation thanks to our rewards credit card. I had to find a bright side somewhere in this moment.

During the 45-minute drive home, Andrew called. "I am sorry my love. I overreacted. Of course, we need to do the surgery." His tone was soft and sweet. "Bodhi is our dog and there is no other choice."

I giggled quietly as he spoke. "I counted on your change of heart," I confided.

I was driving home without Bodhi as the clinic was set for the surgery. Bodhi was spending the night at the veterinary office and was scheduled for the knee repair first thing in the morning.

Bodhi's procedure was successful. The surgeon was stunned, however, by Bodhi's sensitivity to the anesthetics and to pain medications in general. If the staff administered the appropriate dose according to Bodhi's weight, he would remain in a catatonic state for hours. He was responding to very low doses. In fact, he responded best to the typical dose administered to a thirty-pound dog. Given his heightened sensitivities, the veterinarian predicted it could be a longer road to recovery than initially predicted.

It was a full year before Bodhi showed all of the positive results from his knee surgery. Within a year he could walk without compromise, although stairs would forever remain a challenge. We saw structural improvement each day. However, after the surgery, we began to notice dark scabs along his nose. The skin thickened and varied in color from dark black to a whiteish hue. The scabs were itchy and irritated him often. The new symptoms were eventually diagnosed as a canine Lupus. The skin condition would persist, ebbing and flowing according to Bodhi's overall pain levels, for the rest of his life. During damp months, his pain was elevated, and his skin symptoms worsened. With major orthopedic surgery and now an autoimmune diagnosis, our beloved farm successor had a very comprised role.

Samosa understood Bodhi's health challenges. On the days he felt better she wrestled with him more and encouraged him to follow her down the driveway. They would spend the better part of the morning together just enjoying life. When his skin was troublesome and body pain elevated, she entertained herself with solo farm walkabouts. She would come indoors often and nudge his face as a check-in. She would sleep next to him and snore loudly. Bodhi would sigh deeply as her bellowing echoed from the vaulted ceilings, filling the family room in booming tones.

Bodhi's large size created challenges for me. He needed human assistance to help him in and out of the car, as well as in managing certain stairs. Throughout this process, his outdoor interactions lessened. He rarely trekked the entire property. He sought soft and squishy ground to rest on more often than not. Luckily for us, he loved the couch and was easily entertained with cartoons. He found joy and stimulation watching Disney movies. He was especially attentive to the movie *Moana*, which we quickly learned was his favorite show as he would not leave the family room when the film was playing. We enjoyed watching his happy state as he glared at the television, mildly barking when the rooster or pig characters appeared.

"So much for our farm dog." Andrew fought for a seat on the couch, grabbing the remote to change the television station from cartoons. "Bodhi is our couch guard dog."

He gently bent over and kissed Bodhi's head. We were smitten with this dog. Despite the many health challenges and limited responsibilities as a farm guardian successor, Bodhi was a favorite and completely wiggled his way into all of our hearts, cementing our emotions of true adoration.

10
The Nubian Goats

Our dear farmer friends, Kent and Nancy, had been raising Nubian goats for over a decade. I adored their goats and always spent lots of time with them, especially in the spring when the babies were born. After multiple adventures with their herd, it was clear to us all that I needed goats. Perhaps wanted was a better word choice.

"With goats I could recover my farm dream of fresh daily milk," my smile was big, and my vocals fluctuated to a high pitch at the end of my sentence. "I could lessen my use of the weed whacker. Plus, thanks to daily goat milk, I could produce homemade goat cheese and yogurt for us. Once weaned, I could sell the babies and yield a farm profit!"

Andrew rolled his eyes at all of this. He was not impressed with my business presentation and rationale for yet another variety of farm animal. He left the room without a rebuttal, however.

Keema was still living with the herd of horses. The Kune Kunes had been gone for many months. The chickens were vulnerable for the second time. Clearly the new goats would live in ChickenLand and provide protection from predators. Shoot! How could I have forgotten this? It would have been another valid selling point to include in my Nubian goat presentation to Andrew.

After many conversations, Andrew caved. The goats arrived during the winter of 2015. With the help of Kent and Nancy, I selected a mom named Barbie and her baby girl named Valentine from their herd. Mother and daughter were nearly identical. Both were the same brown hue with long white ears and a white patch on their sides. I loved their long and floppy ears and couldn't help but smile as I watched them bounce in the air with each jump they took. I was amazed with Barbie. Although she was not overly affectionate or friendly, she always stared us directly in the eyes. One peep into her horizontal pupils and I knew I was interacting with a unique animal. There was something freaky about the slit shaped pupils—almost alien-like.

Like the Kune Kunes, the goats tolerated Samosa's frequent sniffing of their rear ends. The goats were inquisitive and friendly to all on the farm—humans, chickens, horses, and dogs. While Samosa was intrigued with the goats, Bodhi was in love with them. He could not get enough time with the goats. He pawed at the gate leading into ChickenLand. He eagerly wanted to join the goats in their mini barn. He licked their ears and any part of the body he could get close enough to contact. Barbie did not return his affections. Valentine on the other hand seemed to enjoy her interactions with him. She would often stand on her hind legs, head facing toward him, as a sign of her affection and playfulness. She would fall down, landing on all four legs, and give Bodhi a mild head butt. The two of them had their own interspecies communication and dance.

As winter ended and spring grew near, the buds appeared on the many fruit and nut trees in Chicken-Land. While the goats munched on the grasses when they arrived, they were now nibbling on the fresh sprigs of the edible landscaping. Within two weeks, the trees were pulverized. Andrew tolerated my business adventures and anticipated the day there would be a reward. At this point, there were very few farm benefits.

A weekly trail ride for Andrew brought delight with the horses. We had an abundance of chicken eggs. In their third year of establishment, the fruit trees were just beginning to yield fruit. That is, until the goats ate all of the blossoms! Something had to change before the entire fruit season was a bust.

"The only thing I can think of is electric fencing. The dreaded electric fence!" I moaned.

We had nearly thrown all of the equipment away. During the past two years, we had replaced the electric fence and installed split rail wooden fence around the farm. It was a huge project both physically and financially. No longer being zapped by the electric wire was worth every cent spent though.

"This is going to be difficult. To keep the goats out, we need to incorporate the electric fence to protect the scattered fruit and nut trees." His voice was stern. I could tell he was drawing the electrical grid patterns in his mind as he spoke. "We need to build protection around each tree and connect everything to one solar panel."

Within ChickenLand, the orchards and edible landscaping were planted as smatterings of trees and bushes. There was not a set pattern or flow throughout the half acre. Once again, Samosa watched from under the shade of the cedar tree as Andrew and I clanked the metal post driver to the metal brackets. The sound was deafening. We navigated the terrain and continued pounding posts and pulling heavy gauge wire to each section. The day was long. We were determined to finish and protect the blossoms from any further damage from the goats. As the sun began to set, I was grateful to be done. My hands ached from tugging on the wire and my ears were ready for peace and quiet.

Examining the finished project, one thing came to mind. With the electric fence in place, ChickenLand looked like a giant game of Snafu—a game I had played often on the first MacIntosh computer I had access to as a child. There were electrical wires at varying heights. They zig zagged all around the space. It was a nightmare to walk around, let alone mow. I had to constantly be on the lookout while driving the riding lawn mower, bending like Gumby and contorting my body like the game of Limbo to avoid being shocked. I also had to avoid the nearly invisible electric wire while mowing to prevent being decapitated.

After four months I was over it. The weekly stressors of mowing in such a crazy space overwhelmed me. I had enough of the electrical maze in ChickenLand. It was time to focus on whole herd integration. The horses and Mini Scottish Highland cows did great together. It was time to test the concept with goats!

When we asked our farmer friends about incorporating the goats with the horses, we were encouraged. We learned the expression "got your goat" came from the horse racing tradition. A goat was placed in the horse's stall on the night before each race. The goat provided a calming effect to the high-strung thoroughbred and they were usually instant companions. Plus, with just one stall rental, the horse owner could avoid extra fees he would have incurred had he brought along an equine friend. Often, unscrupulous opponents would steal the goat in the middle of the night which would upset and stress the thoroughbred, causing it to lose the race the next day. Hence the famous phrase, "Got your goat!"

Horses and goats had a long history of mingling well together. Luckily for us, the tradition continued on Fat Dog Farm. Barbie and Valentine were quick to move when the horses requested. It was clear Keema was still boss mare. They would all graze as one big herd in the pasture during the day. The horses returned to the barn and the goats returned to a separate space that housed their mini barn each night. At daybreak, they delighted in morning greetings over a shared fence line. The goats would call out to the horses, and if lucky, a horse or two would respond with a little nicker. As they meandered from their individual barns to the joint pastures, the goats would skip along as the horses trotted to spend the day grazing together in the fields.

Within a week's time, the interspecies herd was adapting and doing well. The electrical nightmare could be disassembled in ChickenLand. Order was restored once again on the farm. Next, I needed to tackle milking. After all, this was the true reason the goats were with us in the first place. Valentine was of weaning age, although she continued to nurse. Valentine was a skittish goat. She was the first to bolt at a sight or sound of something unfamiliar, and she was the first to dart back to the safety of the mini goat barn when the weather turned bad. She was also the last goat to present herself when friends visited the farm or during family gatherings. We concluded through all of her insecurities that she required more nurturing and mothering time. We kept mom and daughter together and hoped to milk Barbie once daily in between Valentine's nursing.

It was July. The heat and humidity of the southeast was in full effect. I had completed daily farm chores and it was now mid-afternoon. No time like the present to try to milk Barbie for the first time. We did not have a milking stand, so milking would require both of us. Andrew and I headed to the goat barn with a small bucket of organic alpha pellets, a glass jar, and the tools and products required to clean and milk the teats. By the time we arrived at the goat barn, we were already sweating. It was nearly ninety degrees in the shade.

Andrew placed his arms under Barbie's belly and held her up. She was a large goat, weighing about one hundred twenty-five pounds, so holding her up was no easy task. I reluctantly crouched underneath her and attempted to milk her. Immediately she squirmed and bleated. Goats bleat when they are distressed. It is a terrible sound, like a crying child. In extreme stress, the bleat sounds are more like a scream. Between the heat, the humidity, the squirming, and the intense goat bleats, I was getting very little milk. As I massaged the teat, the milk simply trickled down the glass jar accumulating to nothing. Andrew was using all of his strength to hold Barbie up. She kept trying to lay down. I knew she should yield a pint of milk since that is what Kent and Nancy were getting each time, they milked Barbie. After we exchanged choice words, Andrew stormed out of the goat house and demanded, "Call Kent!"

"Kent," I muttered in a sheepish voice. "I am not collecting any milk out of Barbie."

Hearing the strain in my tone during my phone call, he sensed my urgency. "I'll be right over!"

This was Barbie's third baby. She had been milked in the past. Although she was not the easiest milker in his herd, she was not labeled as difficult to milk either. Plus, she had high yields. In truth, Kent and Nancy were kind to us. The sale of Barbie, given she was one of their top milk producers, happened only because of our friendship. I knew I should have gathered more milk than a tablespoon this afternoon.

Kent arrived on the farm about thirty minutes later. He hustled to the goat house where she and I were waiting. "I am here to give you an exact tutorial on how to milk Barbie in your own space" he noted with a big smile.

Barbie was happy to discover her old friend. She gazed at him in relaxation and understanding. I, too, felt my shoulders soften and neck tension ease. Kent brought a calming energy to us both. Finally, there would be an expert among us. Barbie and I were both clear on this fact. After his examination, which took less than a minute, he smiled stating, "She's dry."

What? She's dry? I did not understand his words. I had witnessed her yields in the past while visiting Kent and Nancy on their farm. Was she sick?

Easing my fears and confusion, Kent explained light-heartedly, "You are simply trying to milk a goat who does not have any milk right now. Valentine must have nursed all day."

Oh, my goodness, another farm mishap that would have made for quality television. Where was Gwen for this tale? In the worst heat and humidity and in my newness and lack of knowledge, I was milking a goat that had an empty bag. It sure appeared full to me! Clearly, I had no idea what a "full bag" really meant.

It was a story that circulated around the entire farm community. We all laughed and still chuckle over it. I had failed at keeping mini cows in the pasture on several counts. I had failed at breeding pigs, something other swine farmers in the area could not understand. Now, I was milking a dry goat. Perhaps it was time to take my farm badge away. Thankfully we saw humor, not failure.

The next day, Andrew and I had minor success milking Barbie. We did not obtain the pint of milk that we had seen of her yields while at Kent and Nancy's, not even close! I blamed our low totals on my poor technique. I tried talking with farmers, hoping to extract and compile the best milking practices. In truth, it only intimated me. It was second nature to them. Their hands moved in ways their brains were not even registering. How could they give me a step-by-step plan verbally when most of their action was subconsciously ingrained in them? They had been milking animals since they were old enough to carry the stainless-steel pail and small stool into the barnyard each morning. I was at least three decades behind, and I was not certain I could make up the time to gain experience.

August is my least favorite month in the southeast. The sun rays are intense. I spend my time outdoors seeking shade, choosing paths and tasks that are underneath trees and structures. The days are long. The heat and humidity are at their worst. During the month of August, I carefully evaluate farm tasks, postponing anything on the list that can wait until Mid-September or later. After evaluation, specifically in relation to my low yields, milking was now on my postponement list. I no longer had the desire or the passion to become proficient in this daily assignment. Given my frustrations, coupled with the season, it made for a quick and easy decision to abandon the work.

I packed the glass jars and plastic tubing that made up the bulk of my milking set and put the box in the cupboard for later use. I set my intentions for next season. I could picture the many full mason jars in my refrigerator. It was easier to let go of the milking than I had anticipated. I did not feel defeat even though my dreams of homemade goat cheese and goat milk yogurt were squelched. I knew I would master the skill of milking one day.

"After next year's birthing season," I told myself and Andrew. Samosa glared at me from across the room. Her eyes shared her disbelief. "Samosa, I will be a milking machine next year, stop giving me the stank eye." I laughed at loud, sensing her negativity yet feeling confident in my statement. "Next year Samosa, you just wait and see!"

11
Yoshi Bear

Gwen and I had talked about a vacation together for years. We planned several scenarios, yet nothing ever came to fruition. This year was different. Gwen was turning forty. A girls trip was a must. Although she never spoke the words, I knew she understood that even in my fourth year as a farmer, most days I felt overwhelmed. How could I plan a trip for two when I could barely plan the tasks at hand for the next twelve hours? As the saying goes, Gwen took the reins and planned her entire fortieth birthday celebration vacation.

We yearned for sun and beach time. Given we were leaving in January, Florida was the choice for her winter birthday holiday. We planned a four-day adventure. Although Andrew enjoyed the farm, there were still many days he felt engulfed by it. He strongly disliked the monotony of daily rituals like mucking the stalls, filling all water buckets, stuffing hay bags, and feeding the chickens. Leaving him alone on the farm meant I needed to prepare everything in advance. The farm needed to operate like a well-oiled machine while I was away.

Preparing for the endless possibilities for mishap was a daunting task. The fence lines had to be checked and repaired to prevent a breach in security—horses, goats and dogs. All buckets had to be scrubbed clean and all feed bins filled full. There needed to be an abundance of hay. Both chicken coops and the mini goat house needed fresh clean straw. Inside the home, I made sure there was enough dry dog food kibble, wet cat food cans, and extra bully stick treats for Samosa and Bodhi. My life is very habitual. Andrew prefers to go rogue while I am gone. In my opinion, his lack of schedule creates minor chaos for the animals. I tried to combat the dogs' stress by having Andrew give bully stick treats daily.

Sitting on the plane, I was replaying my preparations over the last few days. Had I forgotten anything? Did I need to text Andrew reminders of chores I completed without thought? Tasks that he may be unaware of? I had whispered into each animal's ear, "Please behave yourself while I am away. Please be on your best behavior for your father." I knew if there was one major accident or mishap during his watch that a real estate for sale sign could be waiting for me at the front gates when I returned home.

After easing my worries and calming my overactive mind, I knew the farm was in good hands with Andrew. It was time for me to focus on the joy and peace that was a mere two-hour flight ahead of me. I could not wait for my hands to soak in the ocean. As an acupuncturist, I prided myself on having well-manicured hands. When working with people, I wanted to be certain my skin was soft, nails trimmed, and all calluses removed. Examining my hands now, four years in as a farmer, I did not recognize them. They were rough like sandpaper. My nails were trimmed but varied in length from fingertip to fingertip. I had many scrapes and cuts. I had redness and hangnails around many nail beds. My hands were a mess and in desperate need of the healing ocean waters. Saltwater soaks were in order.

We arrived early in the morning and had the entire day on the beach. The sun was out, but the weather was a little cool. We did not venture into the water, but instead rested on the sand. We reconnected in our conversations and enjoyed reading our books. It was a glorious start to our vacation. I was surprised at how easily and quickly I let go of the farm. I thoroughly enjoyed being in this space of doing nothing.

Unfortunately, the forecast was not on our side. After the first day, a cold front settled into eastern Florida. Rain was predicted for the next few days. Although the days would not be a washout, beach time would be greatly compromised. Not sure what to do in inclement weather, we consulted Google.

"Have you heard of Delray Beach?" I asked Gwen. "Atlantic Avenue is the longest main street in Florida," reading the information directly from Wikipedia. "The street runs through the center of town and extends to the ocean. It's boasted as a popular destination for locals and visitors, with charming streetscapes, shopping, and restaurants."

"It's settled. Let's rent bikes and go," Gwen spoke enthusiastically.

"Bikes, are you crazy? How far is the trek?" I feared the answer.

"I have already found an adventure shop right around the corner from the hotel. Let's go pick up our bikes. This is going to be great!"

We rented bikes from the adventure shop and peddled the twelve and a half miles from Deerfield Beach to Delray Beach for a day adventure. Along the way, Gwen and I realized we were riding on Beachfront Avenue. Middle school memories flooded our minds and hearts as we sang out loud to Vanilla Ice's 'Ice Ice Baby' while pedaling.

"Yo so I continued to A1A Beachfront Avenue

Girls were hot wearing less than bikinis

Rock man lovers driving Lamborghini ...

Ice ice baby, ice ice baby ..."

We delighted in song the entire twelve and a half miles. Gwen was right, the bike ride was a wonderful idea.

Atlantic Avenue was perfect for a cloudy, cool, and lightly rainy day. There were many shops for us to dive into and many streets to explore when the rain ceased. Naturally, we went into a local pet store to purchase souvenir trinkets for Flash, Samosa, and Bodhi. The independently owned pet shop was huge. We explored, snickering at the many sharp-witted plush doggie toys for purchase. It was difficult to select from the StarBarks Frenchie Roast plush toy, the Bark Street Journal newspaper toy, or the Chewy Vuiton Posh purse. This store had it all, and we liked their sense of humor.

As we were laughing and searching for the best gifts, we moved our way to the back of the shop. The funny gifts continued and there were a few puppies for sale too. We oohed and aahed over the precious pooches. They were cute and tiny. Small city dogs—mainly chihuahuas and toy poodles. As we were about to leave, we heard a low toned sound, a muffled growl really. I gazed down and saw a sable colored fluff ball peering up at me. Gwen chuckled. "He's talking to you." Of course, we had to stop and say hello.

He was one pound eight ounces of sheer energy. He was sweet and snuggly and so much fun to play with. He was a mixed breed of toy poodle and Shih Tzu. We interacted with him for a few minutes. We cackled aloud, honoring how poorly suited he would be as a farm dog, appearing more like an overstuffed chipmunk. We left the store without the puppy and without souvenirs for our furry babies.

The next day, I woke early and opened the hotel curtains. The skies were grey. One glance at the ocean and it was clear the winds were whipping creating large white-capped waves. It was going to be another day best suited indoors. Gwen grabbed her phone and began searching the internet.

"I found a nearby yoga studio for a late morning class and there's an Indian food buffet a few yards away from the studio." She knew I would be up for anything as long as Indian cuisine was promised as a fantastic post-workout lunch.

"Great idea! Sign us up." I cheered.

I knew a yoga class was exactly what I needed to stretch and rejuvenate my body. It was also what we both needed to center and calm. Gwen had a lot on her mind. She had recently graduated with a nurse practitioner degree. It was a long journey for her as she continued working as a registered nurse while going to graduate school for the last three years. Her medical boards were scheduled for next month and she was about to turn forty, a decade for which she laughed at me when I turned forty a few years ahead of her.

There were eight of us in the yoga class. It was an intimate room decorated in recycled woods and painted in deep earth tones. The lights were dimmed during the session, making it easy to let go and relax. During each breath, I settled myself, releasing all worries about the farm back home. I felt my shoulders drop, my neck tension soften, and my legs become heavy. Just when I felt like I could fall asleep, I heard the vocals from the adorable puppy the day before. Instead of silence and centeredness, I was hearing his low toned growl. Over and over his sounds replayed in my mind while I could visualize his beady black eyes and fluffy mop-top head staring at me from inside his crate. I could not silence the images and sounds.

After yoga class, I processed my experience with Gwen over a glass of chai tea and a plate of various Indian cuisine delights. I knew the endorphins would kick in soon, thanks to the plethora of Indian spices. Perhaps the food coma of happiness would silence my thoughts of the puppy. The puppy did not invoke sanity in any part of farm life. He was too small and too vulnerable even around a chicken, let alone picturing him near a horse or a tractor.

"Sounds like you are at a crossroad, my friend," Gwen remarked while taking a bite of one of our favorite Indian desserts, Gulab Jamun.

We had been introduced to the dish back in Asheville by our dear friend Ranjeev. He insisted we try them. They were described as spongy milk powder-based desserts shaped in a round ball and soaked in rose scented sugar syrup. "Yuck," was our initial thought. Reluctantly we obeyed Ranjeev's order and fell in love with the scrumptious dessert. From that moment forward, Gwen and I crossed our fingers each time we went to an Indian lunch buffet. Would they have Gulab Jamun? Like a unicorn, they are a rare find. Today, here in Florida, was our lucky day.

"Will you choose cuteness over farm functionality?" Gwen asked with a smile. "Let's go back to Delray Beach this afternoon. You can have a second look."

Gwen was right. I needed clarity and puppy conclusion. When we arrived at the shop, I made a beeline to his cage. Secretly I was hoping Gwen would say, "Yes, let's bring him home," after witnessing his adorable small face again. I know in truth, she brought me here so I could say goodbye to the puppy once and for all.

My whole life I have been more comfortable with animals than humans. On any given day, one can wager I will have watched at least one YouTube video involving some critter—cats, dogs, horses, pandas, raccoons, otters, I have no favorites. Asking me to say goodbye to an animal that has attached to my heart is nearly impossible. Staring at the puppy now, I could feel the tears building in my eyes.

I called Andrew during our Uber ride to Delray Beach after our yoga class and Indian meal.

"Hi love. Guess what I found?" There was a very long pause. I broke the silence. "A fluffy puppy!" I squealed.

He was immediately upset and said sarcastically, "Who finds a puppy on vacation?"

As I replayed Andrew's words in my head, Gwen held my hand and stood next to me as I hugged the puppy tightly one last time. I knew he and Gwen were correct. A dog under ten pounds is not the best selection for a farm. Samosa was eleven and a half years old and a puppy would be the furthest thing on her list of desires. We did not need three dogs. I cried a few tears leaving the pet store that second day. I understood the logic, but my heart was telling me something else.

We enjoyed our remaining days in Florida. Although it was not the sun and beach trip we had yearned for, it was a glorious time away. I was lucky enough to spend several uninterrupted days with one of the people I enjoy most in this world. And, I felt so fortunate to be the person she chose to be with to celebrate this milestone birthday. The many laughs we shared, and the daily outdoor adventures refueled my heart. It was a true holiday where I was able to relax and let go of farm life all while mildly harassing my dearest friend in her fortieth year of life.

Not that I hadn't threatened Gwen the last day of our vacation to do something crazy and throw a wrench in our plans. "This is the last chance to grab the puppy," I shouted upon hearing our flight was delayed over an hour at the West Palm Beach Airport. "I believe we have enough time to take an Uber and purchase the puppy. It's a sign Gwen, the flight delay means I should claim him."

I vocalized with more fluctuation in my voice than I meant. After all, I did not mean to ask it as a question. Wasn't it more of a statement?

"We are not going. I am not going to be responsible for your divorce." Her statement was firm. She sensed my hesitation and knew to put a kibosh on my plan once and for all.

When Andrew picked me up from the airport, he asked, "So where's the puppy?"

Shocked, I responded by restating his words. "You declared, I better not pick you up at the airport and see a puppy with you." I gave him a glare of confusion.

"Since when do you listen to me?" he grinned.

Two weeks post-vacation and I was still talking about the puppy. Andrew rolled his eyes each time. He allowed me to finish my tale of the few special interactions I had with the puppy while in Florida. Finally, one day he noted, "You are just like the ad from the Volkswagen commercial! The ad showing two people in a car sales parking lot and only one Jetta car remaining."

I knew this commercial and the ending. As one of the buyers quickly and deliberately licks the door handle of the car, it is clear from the facial expressions of the second buyer that the licking behavior signals the Jetta had been claimed. "You have energetically licked the puppy!" He laughed and growled at the same time.

Perhaps he was right. I called the shop, inquiring if the puppy was still available. To my complete surprise, he was. Luckily, I had prepared a list of questions to ask prior to my call. I was aware of puppy mills and inhumane breeders. I needed answers before making my decision. I asked, "Who was the breeder? What is your relationship with the breeder? What were the breeding conditions and where were the parent dogs?"

I also asked for the exact breeder contact information for my own investigation. After much research, I was convinced he was the correct choice to be our next dog.

For the third time since purchasing the farm, Andrew picked up an animal during a business trip. This time he had a solar project to visit near the southern Alabama state line. A mere seven extra hours of driving and he would have the puppy. I say "mere" as for me, seven hours in a car is torturous. I am extremely fidgety after four hours. My attitude turns foul and there is no amount of quality music or enough snacks to make the time pass quickly. Given that Andrew travels constantly for his work, a car trek is like a stroll in the park for him.

On this trip though, the puppy would have to spend an extra few days on the road with Andrew. Andrew was certain the landowners he was connecting with would enjoy playing with a puppy. "Besides, the puppy is two pounds and hypoallergenic. How inconvenienced could one be with this little guy?" He winked as he booked his flight to Florida.

The trip was a success. In just two short days on the road, the new puppy had wiggled his way to his place as top dog in Andrew's heart. He called from the road sharing similar tales of joy being with the new little guy. I could not wait for him to return home.

Samosa did not agree with our decision. In fact, she wouldn't even acknowledge the puppy during their interactions. The puppy tried very hard to please her. He wiggled his tail, made many low tone vocals, stood on his hind legs, licked her fur, and even followed her around the farm in obedience. Still, she would not even peek at him. She acted as if he was invisible, although she was never mean to him. She never pounced on him or flipped him over. Her attitude was more a feeling that she could not be bothered with such a useless creature.

Bodhi was intrigued by the new puppy from the comfort of the couch. He enjoyed watching the high energy fluff ball dart around the living room. Bodhi and the puppy played games of chase daily. The puppy loved to jump all over Bodhi's body while he was laying down. Bodhi and Samosa played with lots of rumble and tumble. Bodhi now adapted his play, being aware of the puppy's size and fragility. Bodhi was gentle with his mouth, easy with his paws, and very attuned to his large size. It was amazing to watch Bodhi play tough with Samosa and then delicately with the puppy.

The puppy needed a name. Gwen and I had referred to him as Boris DelRay while in Florida. Once home, the name did not seem fit him. The puppy was high energy, comical, and fluffy—a bit of a spaz really. Andrew referred to him as Major Happiness because that was his dominant emotion. We finally settled on Yoshi Bear.

Yoshi is the Japanese word for "lucky one." Yoshi was darn lucky to be living with us on the farm. Plus, we were lucky to have him.

Many of our friends feared for Yoshi's life. He was now three pounds and vulnerable to everything required in farm operations. We made sure to train him to run away from the bobcat. We instilled in him to scamper away from the goats when they approached, but more importantly, to come to us when large trucks appeared in the driveway. We were not worried about a farm accident, nor a Yoshi death. We were training him to be a farm-savvy small dog.

Three weeks on the farm and an accident happened. I was letting the horses out of the barn that morning. All the dogs joined me in this adventure. I had lost sight of Yoshi as we walked from the barn outside to the large paddock. I assumed Yoshi ran back to the house. After all, Andrew was inside sipping on his morning coffee. Yoshi had returned to the house a few times before to be on the couch with Andrew rather than taking part in morning farm duties. Suddenly, I heard a screech. The type of sound that you will never fully release from your memory. The shrill that immediately causes your heart to skip a beat and your body to breakout into a full sweat.

I panicked. Where was Yoshi? With so many horse legs and horse hooves to navigate, my eyes were lost in the chaos of that moment. Then I saw him. Yoshi was lying flat and trembling. It was clear my mare had stepped on him. I screamed for Andrew. As I scooped him up, guilt filled my body. How could I have allowed such an accident to happen? I felt frantic. What if Yoshi's spine was crushed in the accident? All negative emotions were flooding my system simultaneously. My brain told me we had no business having such a small dog on a farm. He was sure to die. In just a few short weeks my mare had stepped on him. I feared we were off to the veterinary emergency clinic for major surgery, best case scenario. Euthanasia as the worst case.

I fully understand why I was never interested in emergency medicine. I am not good at staying focused under high stress. I do not come up with solutions or remedies under pressure. I had Yoshi in my arms but was so focused on my stupidity with purchasing him that I was not focused on him and his behaviors. Thank goodness Andrew was home. Like a robot, I was heading to the car for the trek up the mountain for medical evaluation. It was Andrew who noticed Yoshi's movement.

"Yoshi is moving. He's fairly normal for the accident that just occurred. Bring him in the house," he stated calmly.

Once inside, we began our assessment. I was able to palpate his abdomen. I could move all four of his legs and paws. I could lift his head and his ears. None of these examinations created pain or any reaction from Yoshi, although he was still trembling. We presumed these were residual emotions of fear. He continued to peer at us with a blank stare, a look of innocence in those beady little black eyes.

I released a few tears as the high threat situation settled. We gave Yoshi a homeopathic remedy, Arnica Montana, for pain and inflammation. We could not believe he was alright. Andrew investigated the accident site. Fortunately, it appeared that my mare had stepped on Yoshi in a sandy, squishy ground of the paddock and she was unshod. There were no metal horseshoes on her to create an even greater impact. Within an hour, Yoshi was behaving normally. He was darting around the property displaying glee and glory, as per usual.

Post-accident, Yoshi moved with greater quickness and mindfulness around the horses. He learned to pay closer attention to human movements and car tires too. He became hypersensitive to many environments, especially by learning to avoid all situations where he could be squashed. Thank goodness that was the one and only major farm accident with him. He was, and continues to be, our savvy small farm dog after all.

12
Great Loss

Yoshi was acclimating well into the pack of now three. He was potty trained, and he only chewed one pair of shoes and a small corner of molding in the hose. We felt fortunate to have survived the bulk of puppyhood with little damage. Yoshi enjoyed his daily adventures with Bodhi and Samosa. He played the game of chase each morning with Bodhi, and then headed outside to follow his pack leader. He would dash behind Samosa with his tongue hanging out in glee. He had an extra wag or two in his tail during those walks. Samosa simply tolerated his presence.

There were times when we would laugh at her sense of humor. Samosa would lead Yoshi into predicaments he was not savvy enough to avoid. She would take him into the woods where he would get trapped in a briar patch. His fluffy hair would tangle, and he would become paralyzed. We would hear high pitched yelping sounds and have to go to his rescue. One day, while we were installing wooden fencing, we heard Yoshi frantically barking. Searching everywhere we could not find him. I began to feel anxious and panicked as we examined the two-acre pasture yet had zero sight of him.

"Found him!" Andrew shouted with joy.

As I approached, Andrew and I noticed Yoshi had fallen down one of the three-foot holes we had dug over a year ago for the wooden posts. Samosa was standing over the hole, grinning as she guarded him.

We knew her antics were from humor. After all, if she really wanted him gone, given the sixty-pound size difference, she could end his life in a single bite. She seemed to me to channel her feelings of under-appreciation of him into big sister pranks. As Samosa's movements slowed and she became less physically active, she transferred that energy into mental stimulation. This was clear from the many tricks she played on the ten-month-old puppy who idolized her.

During one of Paul's visits, he called to say, "It's not the horses this time that are in my way with the bobcat. Rather, you need to come out to the pasture and collect Yoshi."

Paul had seen Samosa lead Yoshi down the driveway and into the pasture directly in front of his work with the bobcat bucket. Samosa moved out of the working path but kept her sidekick in direct line.

As the late summer months progressed, we noticed Samosa reducing her daily rituals. Yoshi no longer spent the mornings following her as she checked the fence line; Samosa now simply managed the driveway. She slept most of the day, lying in the shade on the cool ground in a bed of fescue grass. When the windows were open, we could hear her snoring from any room in the house. Her interest in farm life and farm protection continued unbated, though. On days she felt good, she would bark at anything that flew overhead. She discovered a new fondness for guarding the front gate. It was an easy walk down to the front gate where she could survey all who entered the farm.

Samosa thoroughly enjoyed the fall due to cooler weather, shorter days, and most importantly for her, hunting season. During October, she would spend great amounts of time in the woods, searching for abandoned carcasses. Andrew and I dreaded hunting season. I disliked hearing the gunshots, especially while trail riding. I was sure to ride after prime hunting hours and to wear brightly colored clothing. While out for the day, I mentally prepared to witness clusters of deer, frantically seeking safety somewhere in the woods. But worse than all of this for me were the yearly fall finds that Samosa would bring home.

It started the very first month we moved to the farm in 2011. Samosa had been on a walkabout for several hours. As she returned, we noticed Captain and Dutchess snorting and running around the pasture. It was clear from their body language and the energy exerted that they were on high alert. Glancing out the window we spotted Samosa in a light jog coming up the driveway. She was dragging something, so I sent

Andrew out to investigate. The horses' reactions were justified. The smell of rotting flesh was intense as Andrew approached her. Samosa had a deer's large intestine hanging from her mouth. She coveted her find and dug a hole for it near the cedar tree for safe keeping. I swallowed hard and plugged my nose with my thumb and pointer finger, making sure not to throw up while patting her head. "You are no longer a city dog, are you?" I couldn't help but smile as the words came out, sensing her satisfaction and joy.

The second year on the farm during hunting season, Samosa returned with yet another body part. Once again, I saw her jogging up the driveway. She was strutting and grinning. Knowing what she found the year before, I sent Andrew out to meet her. This year she brought the entire hind leg of a deer—bone, hoof, and fur included. She carried this treasure around the farm daily for the next month. I was relieved to see the leg shrinking in size until ultimately one day she was finished chewing on her delight and the piece vanished.

Her third year was less graphic. Samosa would appear from the forest with various deer bone fragments. Luckily, most of these disintegrated quickly as the parts were small and easily consumed. I did not witness her carrying bones around the farm each day as happened the year before.

During her fourth year of hunting season rewards, we had a break from the deer family. This year she simply found one box turtle shell. She would stick her tongue through the middle of the shell and carry it around like a human placing a roll of toilet paper over their pointer finger. She would trot through the fields bringing her shell along to accompany her on her daily adventures.

2016 marked our fifth year on the farm. Samosa was a few weeks shy of her twelfth birthday. Her walkabouts were greatly reduced, in part to her slowing gait. She spent the bulk of her days sleeping, not searching.

"I think we can assume to be clear of hunting remains this year." We were sipping on our coffee with the patio door opened. Samosa was snoring around the corner, and the low tones were ricocheted off of the ceiling as I spoke. "What a relief!"

"You are not going to believe this!" Andrew was in Texas working on a large wind project. I called to share my surprise. "Samosa came home snarling at Yoshi as he approached her. She was holding a bone in her mouth! I didn't even notice she left the pasture today."

This would not be the only day she returned with a cherished find. Her most adored of the season was a deer jawbone, equipped with a row of teeth and all. What made these episodes extra incredible was they were found in spite of her ailing health. During the beginning of the month, Andrew noticed a small growth on her left shoulder. It felt fleshy to the touch, was red in its skin color, and was the size of a grape. She was not bothered when we touched it or when we poked the skin of the area around it. She was eating and drinking normally, and her mood was good. We decided to keep an eye on it.

In less than a week's time, the growth increased to the size of a small tangerine. She was licking the skin of the area often. She would whimper at times and seemed agitated. We took her to the veterinarian who believed she may have been bitten by a snake. That made sense, especially given her two deer bone finds in the woods the week prior. She could have easily been bitten during one of those walkabouts. We were sent home with antibiotics.

After three days the mass continued to grow. Samosa was now pacing the house and licking the growth continually. I returned to the veterinarian for a second visit where the mass was biopsied. Samosa was sent home with a steroid and a charge to continue the antibiotics. I left the appointment feeling nervous and anxious. It would be a week before the lab results and pathology report came back.

Andrew was out of town on business travel. I was home alone, and my traumas with Remmie's passing replayed in my mind all too often. Remmie had seemed to be feeling a little under the weather for about a week in February. She was sleeping more and had a rattling sound in her throat, yet she was a smashed face pug and rattling facial sounds were all too common in her world. Andrew returned one weekend from Philadelphia and we took Remmie for a saunter around the block that Saturday night, hoping to revive her spirits.

She stopped often, protesting moving any further. As a roly-poly pug, this was not an uncommon behavior either. When Andrew left that weekend, we had assumed Remmie had a mild case of the winter blues. Perhaps even a virus. She was a little lazier than normal, yet she had turned twelve two weeks previously.

Two days later, I returned home from work at 5 p.m. to find a pug greeting me in the doorway who was double the size of that morning. Her breathing was very labored. She was in pain, a strain expressed through her eyes. I rushed her to the veterinary office. She was in congestive heart failure and needed to be euthanized immediately. I was shocked and traumatized. I was also alone.

Now again, I was alone in the house as Samosa's health appeared to be deteriorating rapidly. She was still engaged in daily life, and so I continued to have false hopes. The week of the biopsy report is when she brought home her third find, the deer jawbone. She was very proud of this. She snarled at both Bodhi and Yoshi when they tried to investigate it. She kept the jawbone all to herself and carried it from place to place. Even in these moments, I could not deceive myself. Knowing her as well as I did, I knew there was no denying how terrible she felt. She paced more than ever. I felt paralyzed, for no matter what healing remedies and healing modalities I used, her pain was elevated.

I was living in terror. I cried more than I smiled. I was restless each night. Samosa would pace the bedroom, irritated by the lump in her skin. I would lie awake in misery watching her anguish. My mind ran away with me, envisioning dark scenarios. I was in agony knowing there was little I could do to ease her discomfort. The only thing I knew to do was keep her cool. She felt best in cold weather. Each night I turned the air conditioning down to 60 degrees. I went to bed wearing wool socks and a thick cotton hoodie sweatshirt underneath a down comforter, hoping she would find at least a little comfort and peace.

When the veterinarian called with the lab results, I was mentally prepared for her words and for the bad news. The growth on Samosa had increased yet again in the five short days. The veterinarian declared Samosa had a mast cell tumor and less than forty-eight hours to live. My stomach sank and tears poured from my eyes. I lost my voice and I had no words when I hung up the phone. Samosa came over to me, nosing my leg with her three low toned grunts. In my deepest trauma and in her final hours, she was comforting me.

Andrew returned from a wind energy project in North Dakota late that Friday night. The veterinarian stated Samosa would not survive through the weekend, and she would experience severe pain and even greater agitation with each passing hour. "With the whole family together, let's plan to have our last Saturday morning before taking her to the clinic to be put to sleep this afternoon." As I spoke to Andrew there was a big lump in my throat making it very difficult to get the words out.

"It's going to be a tough morning. Let's walk with Samosa one last time around the property." Tears were collecting in Andrew's eyes too. Samosa was very intentional that morning. She slowly moved through the pasture checking the parts of the fence line she could reach with the least amount of effort. She was in much pain shown with each difficult and shaky step she took. She meandered over to each horse and paused. Rather than running from her, as they had in the past many times during Samoa's game of chase, the horses halted and returned her gaze. She sauntered back to the house and touched her nose to each cat. Bodhi was by her side that entire morning as she said goodbye to all on the farm. Yoshi was darting around the pasture, clueless to the somber energy of the day.

"This is never going to be easy. No time is right. We have to go." My voice was flat. I forced us into the car. As we drove down our long driveway, Samosa looked out the window. It was an eerie feeling. She was clearly taking her last view of the farm. She was in the moment and very aware of what was happening.

Again, the tears burst from my eyes. I could not see to drive, and I was grateful when Andrew took the wheel. Samosa had dictated her last few hours on the farm. She set the pace, she determined the path, and it was she who initiated individual goodbyes to all. Now I had to get over myself. I had to relinquish my fear and misery. It was time I honor her with my own goodbye.

The staff at the emergency clinic was exquisite. They took us into a room that had floor to ceiling windows, overlooking a beautiful garden. The bandage material used for her IV was the color red for love. The sticky gauze was cut into the shape of a heart. As the veterinarian administered the fluid, Samosa grunted her playful sounds and stared into our eyes. We laid with her. We caressed her fur and shared many words of praise and of our adoration to her. The time ticked by slowly. Suddenly, she jolted and glanced over her shoulder to look behind her. Then, she quickly settled. Soon after that moment, she passed.

During the drive home, through many tears and slurred speech, Andrew inquired, "Who do you think was in the room with Samosa?"

"It was clear she saw someone else in the room with us. It was freaky and absolutely amazing," I commented in wonder.

Samosa was surprised by her vision but calmed in her knowing. It was a profound moment. Andrew and I assumed the man who adored her for the first five years of her life was also at her side. Six years prior to her passing, that man committed suicide. Samosa was with him in his final hour. We believe he was with Samosa in hers.

I was a walking zombie for days. The serious misfortune that had played in my mind for so many nights had finally arrived. The sadness I felt was deeper than that of my loss of Remmie. Remmie had been a companion through my troubled young adulthood. Samosa was my soul sister. Samosa and I did not play games. We did not go out for social outings at dog parks. We did not play fetch. What we did was simply just be.

In our six short years together, Samosa and I spent most of our time reviving our souls. We were both awakened through the farm, a life changing event for us. The farm was the environment that nourished a new understanding of who we truly were.

"Humankind is being led along an evolving course, through this migration of intelligences, and though we seem to be sleeping, there is an inner wakefulness that directs the dream, and that will eventually startle us back to the truth of who we are."

~ Rumi (*The Essential Rumi*)

In many moments, I find myself standing on the farm, and I pause. I take the time to view the pastures. I gaze up at the sky above, paying attention to each bird. I stop and become hyperaware of feeling the breeze on my face and the earth beneath my feet. I know that Samosa is forever alive in me, especially on her farm. I am in awe of her and continue to love her deeply each day. She is and will always be one of my greatest soul companions. I am grateful her essence lives on in us and in and through the Fat Dog Farm brand, which immortalizes her silhouette.

13
Liverachi and Subi

We attended the New Year's Eve celebration in our small town of Tryon. Each year, Main Street is closed with barricades blocking traffic for several blocks, and individual fire pits are placed down the centerline for kids to gather around and roast marshmallows. The local plaza is buzzing with the festivities, with less than a thousand people in attendance. A live band plays the sounds of the seventies, and to ring in a new year, Andrew and I, surrounded by a few friends, were out on the dance floor grooving to the classic "Play That Funky Music." I found joy in this one moment, despite the continued heartache with Samosa's passing. I was ready to ring in 2017 and let go of the severe grief felt from the last few months. I listened to the bass, swayed my hips, and danced the sadness away.

The next morning, after an evening of smiles and lightheartedness, I found clarity. For the first time in two months, the dense fog that weighed heavy on my mind from missing my furry best friend was beginning to lift. I sat on the couch sipping coffee, admiring Bodhi who was watching morning cartoons. My shoulders sank, my chest released, and the furrow between my eyes dissipated. I was able to find joy snuggled next to Bodhi compared to feeling uneasy in the "something is missing" sensations that had been plaguing me. In this newly discovered space, I recognized that I needed a farm focus to occupy me in the new year. Given my history, tackling milking was a tall order. I felt able to dive into the all-consuming task.

Pulling the basket off of the top shelf in the coat closet, I pillaged through the chaos. Mis-matched gloves filled most of the bin. As I sorted through the mess, seeking a pair of mittens and warm scarf to wear for morning chores, I heard Yoshi running around the family room rug. He was tossing one of Andrew's leather work gloves. It must have fallen out during my search, and Yoshi was thoroughly enjoying his find. I laughed and said, "Come on you two, it's a new year with a new chore to consider. Let's go see the goats."

We now had three Nubians. A few weeks before Samosa's seriously failing health, we had brought home a young male goat. There was little time to enjoy him because shortly after he arrived Samosa's tumor developed and was all consuming in my life. As I stared at this young boy goat now, this early morning with Yoshi and Bodhi by my side, I had an opportunity to reflect. I had missed his actual birth by just under an hour last June. On that day, I had stopped in to visit with Kent and Nancy after an herbal conference I attended in Black Mountain, NC. Our friendship with Kent and Nancy centered around our adoration of

Nubian goats and farm life in general. We also connected over alternative health concepts, functional medicine, and holistic remedies. I was excited to share all I had learned earlier that day, including a few recipes from the herbal kitchen.

Nancy was out running errands. Kent and I chatted about herbal formulas while visiting his goats. Although most of the kids had been born the week prior during this birthing season, he still had one remaining pregnant goat. Given her size, we were certain she was due any day. As we approached his goat barn, we knew something was off.

"Lipstick has clearly delivered a kid," Kent said with eyebrows furrowed, "but there is not a kid near her." Frantic for a moment, we both searched for the baby. "There it is, near the creek."

From our assessment, it appeared as if Lipstick delivered next to a ridge. The kid goat tumbled down the embankment. He was less than an hour old and nestled into the tall grasses and reeds near the small creek. Head down and grazing, Lipstick was unattached and unfazed by her loss.

Kent and I held the baby boy goat and reintroduced mama to her newborn son. It was a tender moment. Since that hour, I had always been especially fond of that new baby. He was a liver brown chestnut color with a black face and black colorations on his leg. All of his markings were in balance and beautifully proportioned.

He was sweet, quiet, and calm. He was also aloof and independent. I assumed these traits to be a direct reaction to his birth experience. We called him Liverachi in honor of his color and dramatic flair. At weaning age, I brought him home to our farm to be with our two female Nubian goats.

"Why do we need a male goat?" Andrew scowled in agitation. "We can take our females to Kent and Nancy's for breeding!"

We had discussed this during our goat business planning stage a year ago. I had lovingly referred to the yearly event as "Pregnancy Camp." We would keep our herd small, two to three female goats. During the month of October, we would send the females to Kent and Nancy's farm for a month-long stay. At the time of the original discussion, the plan was fool proof. I had not meet Liverachi though.

In August, Liverachi was two months old. He was young and still intact. Given his coloration, Kent thought he would render a quality breeding goat and thus had not neutered him. Outside of Andrew, all beings on the farm were sterile. Myself included. I had a tubal ligation at twenty-five years old. Baby free, no matter which species in our home, had been set in stone since our first date. We sat at the bar in Laughing Seed, Asheville's original downtown vegetarian restaurant. As we sampled our hummus trio and spinach dip appetizers, I blurted out loud, "Just so you know I am fixed and can't have kids."

"That's a lot of information. I thought we would simply share an appetizer and go from there." Andrew laughed with a strained look on his face. Mind you this was our very first date. I wanted to be upfront and honest. Perhaps I was too hasty in sharing this information.

Breeding has never been on the docket, outside of raising chicks. This alone was the strongest reason not to bring Liverachi home. Yet, during his initial hours of life, I bonded with him. I wanted him on the farm and rationalized, "We can allow him to have one set of kids and then have him neutered." Enthusiastically, I laughed, "Like the importance of roosters in a flock of hens, I believe male yang energy is important even in our small herd of female goats."

"But bucks are very stinky. Their strong musky odor is nasty. You know they spray urine on their faces and beards to attract the ladies!" Andrew spoke with his nose crinkled and forehead furrowed. "Neither of us are a fan of the male musk odor," he reminded me.

"I agree, my love. I promise after a quick breeding season; I will have him gelded ASAP." I was confident that having Liverachi neutered at a young age would greatly reduce the possibility of any nasty boy goat odor on the farm.

During the week of Christmas, we witnessed Liverachi mounting both Barbie and Valentine on numerous occasions. He was young and had one thing on his mind. It was clear from his prolific actions that he needed to be neutered soon. Luckily for us, there was a veterinary clinic twenty minutes from the house that worked with goats. Given he was six months old, nearly forty-five pounds, and that it was winter, the surgery needed to be performed inside the clinic. I made the appointment for early Monday morning, knowing Andrew would be in town to help. To our surprise, Liverachi easily loaded into the backseat of the Tacoma truck. Andrew lifted him from the ground and placed him on my lap. He did not even squirm or try to escape. Andrew closed the back door and jumped into the driver's seat. I packed the backseat with old blankets and towels. I wrapped Liverachi in layers, fearing bathroom activities while he was inside the automobile.

Liverachi melted into my lap and simply stared out the window during the journey. He was calm as he gazed at the sights along the road. For a moment I heard a ukulele and the chorus for "Somewhere Over the Rainbow" playing in my ear as we drove on the winding countryside roads like we were out for a Sunday drive. That is, until we came to stoplights. Noting the smiles on people's faces in the cars next to us snapped me back into reality. We were traveling with a goat. A goat inside the truck!

As with his overall demeanor, Livercahi seemed unaffected by the surgery. The procedure was fast and successful. The car ride home was just as simple. Once back on the farm, he joined the females and carried on about his day. Only time would tell if Liverachi's mating behavior prior to his surgery would bring fertility success.

Liverachi was a playful goat. It was not uncommon to see him leaping through the fields, encouraging the girl goats to interact with him. He befriended all of the horses but, was especially fond of Keema. He nuzzled her often and was seen chewing grass by her side most days. She did not return his affections, but she did tolerate his obsessive attentions.

In his youth and thereby small size, Liverachi was an escape artist. He often slid through the split rail fence and could be found chewing the vegetable plants in my garden and eating ornamental bushes around the house. Chasing him back through the fence was a common occurrence.

It was Valentine's day and Andrew left early that morning to run errands. When he returned, I watched as he pulled a horse trailer up the driveway. Excitement filled my body and I ran out the front door to wrap him in a hug and kisses of gratitude. Finally, we could move the animals as needed. I could not wait to trailer a horse over and ride with some of my dear friends. I snatched my mare out of the pasture and signed up for a group riding lesson at Three Gables Farm just a few miles down the road. I heard extra noises coming from the trailer that day as I traveled slowly along the windy country road. I thought to myself, "Boy is she excited to go to class."

As I pulled into the farm, everyone was already riding in the arena. Jennifer was riding her gelding Hombre, Pam was on her mare, Karina, and Georgie was riding her mare, Cami. I had the windows down as I drove into the farm. I could hear Jennifer shouting to me from inside the arena, "Quite a ruckus coming from your trailer today."

Once parked, I walked to the rear of the trailer to pull down and drop the ramp so I could off load my mare. As the ramp lowered, Jennifer and I heard, "Baa baa baa." Startled by the unusual sound, I dropped the ramp and saw Liverachi. He was standing in the trailer! How did he get there? More importantly, how did I miss him as I loaded my mare? These mysteries remain.

We tried to continue with riding class, leaving Liverachi in the trailer to munch on hay. After two minutes, it was clear that was going to be unacceptable. I had closed all of the doors in the trailer to ensure he could not escape. As the four of us rode in the arena for class, we could hear the bellows from the goat. The sounds ricocheted around in the closed trailer, and the acoustics made his vocals seem twice as vibrant. Several of the horses became frightened. They were certain there was a lion in the trailer, ready to pounce on them at any moment. It was clear Liverachi needed to return home ASAP. Thank goodness that was his one and only unplanned adventure off of the farm.

It was near Andrew's birthday, the end of March, when the signs became clear. We felt confident both Barbie and Valentine were pregnant. Barbie was the first to show. This would be her fourth baby, and her body had muscle memory from her past pregnancies. She had expanded sides as well as a protruding lower abdomen early in her gestation. Valentine was just a year old. She was slightly rounder, but one needed to strain their eyes to be certain of a pregnancy bump. We were on the gestation countdown and hypothesized both were due the end of May.

We were excited, although subconsciously we were somewhat pessimistic. We had been in this place multiple times before with the Kune Kunes pigs and each time we had been wrong. A part of our awareness worried that the goats were just fat. Still, I marked the days off on the calendar and wished time away. I was hopeful that this time our kids would be born.

It was April. Spring was in full bloom. Any adventure off the farm meant rolling down all of the windows in the car. I thoroughly enjoyed using all of my senses while taking the sights, sounds, feel, and smells of spring in the Foothills. After the bland colors of winter, I always enjoy seeing the Bradford pear trees in full white bloom, with smatterings of weeping cherries and their pink flower blossoms. There are always numerous daffodils and hyacinths in all fields to behold and many azaleas in rays of pinks, magentas, and whites. This day in particular was extra warm. It was a glorious day to run errands and see the beauty in the countryside.

Upon returning home, as I drove up the driveway, I could hear Valentine call out. It was not the usual greeting of hello. This was a distress call. Once parked, I immediately went to her. She was alone in the goat barn. As I approached her, I noticed blood on the fur of her chest. Something was wrong. To my horror, she had miscarried two kids in the goat barn. They were about six weeks premature. She had cleaned the babies and now nuzzled them. She was mourning and wanted me to witness her heart's distress.

I sat on the floor of the goat barn comforting her, but I was also caressing her to comfort me. I shed many tears. She oscillated between nudging the babies and seeking solace from me. We stayed in this place for at least thirty minutes. My heart experienced an array of emotions. I was in awe of her awareness and need to connect with her human in her distress. I was sad for her loss. I was once again acutely aware of the brutal realities and challenges faced all too often in farm life.

The next day was a typical day on the farm. Valentine was with the other goats, spending the day grazing with the horses. All activities resumed as if yesterday were an event that happened decades ago. The heaviness felt from the day before was absent. We found joy knowing Barbie was about a month from delivering.

Entering the month of May, Barbie was as wide as she was tall. We jokingly called her an Oompa Loompa from the characters in the movie *Willy Wonka and the Chocolate Factory*. We were on daily lookout for a delivery. I hiked into the pastures several times each day investigating for labor signs. I used a flashlight for night checks, looking for signs of delivery before bed. After weeks of hovering, I finally realized she was going to have the baby unrelated to my obsessive behaviors and micromanagement.

We had been out for supper with friends Friday, May 19, 2017. We relished our evening out, eating glorious foods, laughing, and drinking wine. It took us back to our days in Asheville. We let go of the farm for over two hours and quickly found our city folk groove. It was a late return from our dinner outing. We played with the dogs, and I checked the horses around 10 p.m. that night. My belly was full from great foods and a little too much wine. I was feeling lazy and tired, so I decided not to grab the flashlight for Barbie's bedtime goat check.

As I ambled back to the home, I shouted, "Goodnight Barbie."

I knew my sentiments would reach to the goat barn. To my surprise, a high pitched "Baa baa" returned my call. I knew immediately the sound was not from Liverachi, Barbie, or Valentine. This sound was from a newborn kid. I ran to the house screaming, "Andrew get out here!"

My shouts were in delight, but they were loud. Had our neighbors been closer, all would have been startled awake from my ecstatic calls as I ran back to the house to collect Andrew. He grabbed the flashlight and the camera, and we rushed to the goat barn. Once inside, a newly cleaned kid filled our sights and immediately won over our hearts. Barbie had delivered about twenty minutes prior without complication. She had a doe.

We had the perfect name for her. Our friends from dinner had a ten-year-old boy. He was their third child, the baby who was ten years younger than his two older brothers. His older brothers both drove Subarus. One day, Ben and his mother Theresa and I were all sizing up Barbie, eager to see signs of delivery. We could not wait to play with a baby goat and discussed all of the upcoming joy we would feel. As we talked about the unknown kid, Ben declared that we needed to name the goat Subi in tribute to his big brothers. On the evening wc were sharing a glorious meal with the Thompsons, it seemed to be the perfect sign; the new little doe was to be called Subi.

Subi looked like Liverachi. She had his black dorsal stripe and camouflaged brown ears. She had the black markings on all four of her legs. There was little that resembled her mother. As his one and only baby, we felt proud on Liverachi's behalf. We stayed in the goat barn for nearly an hour that evening. The air was filled with excitement.

After five and a half years on the farm, we finally had our first breeding success. We went to bed very late that night with a glow in our eyes and huge smiles on our faces. A sense of accomplishment washed over us. It was a long journey, for us to finally feel these positive emotions. Where the road had been paved with bricks of disappointment, naivety, incompetence, and ignorance, it was now a glowing, golden brick road of joy, contentment, and peace in this one doe birth. Bodhi and Yoshi had been in the goat barn that evening too. Barbie was wonderful in allowing early introductions of her newborn to the dogs. The whole farm witnessed the glory of Subi's birth.

After midnight, when the happiness and adrenaline from the hours prior released, I went to bed thinking of Samosa. I knew she was with us in spirit that evening, too. I could detect her face. I noticed her soulful eyes staring at me and that she was wearing a smile. She would have been excited this day. Fat Dog Farm was as much her vision as it is ours. Each failure and each success is shared in her heart too. That night, Samosa smiled from above. That night I heard her howls of joy replay in my mind and vibrate in my heart as I fall fast asleep.

14
Milking

During the first two days Barbie and Subi remained in the goat barn. Subi ventured little and she seemed to be simply taking in all the sights the world was offering her in this new space. She let us touch her, and I visited often. She tolerated me taking an insane number of photos of her within the first forty-eight hours of her birth. The days were sunny and warm, with lovely, cool nights. Subi was quite comfortable, and it was clear for her calm demeanor, shiny coat, and expanding belly that she was flourishing.

Barbie, on the other hand, was not as comfortable. She was producing a lot of milk. Subi was only drinking a little during this early stage of life. It was clear from her compromised movements that we needed to drain some milk. A year ago, I thought I knew what a full bag of milk looked like. Watching Barbie now, I could not have been more wrong. It was abundantly clear that Barbie's bag was overly full. Her fur and skin had the appearance of a balloon that was about to pop. Her skin glistened in its tautness—the full expansion of her tissues. She moved cautiously and she required extra care while standing and lying down. In fact, she greatly struggled to lie down.

We did laugh at poor Barbie's expense. "Can you imagine if we had to go to bed and fall asleep while lying on top of a yoga ball!" I giggled, but knew she was miserable.

It was time once again to milk Barbie. I last attempted this nine months ago. Hesitant and unconfident, I referred to the task as "Milking Part Deux." Like an iPhone update, I had hoped that all of my errors were now magically resolved. Once again, we had our milking tools and glass mason jar. We headed to the goat barn. As we hustled toward their house, I said to Andrew, "I am certain Barbie will smell my anxieties from a mile away."

Barbie glared at us as we entered her space. She knew what was coming. She let out a stressful "BAAAAA."

After a brief pause and our collective countdown, "1, 2, 3... Go!" Andrew quickly leapt in her direction wrapping his arms around her belly. He held her up, working hard to hold her steady so I could attach the milking equipment. After a few awkward moments, and a few distress calls from Barbie, we were having success.

"Look, love, milk is running down the mason jar." I laughed out loud. "Compared to our last experience, this milk is gushing out." After a mere ten minutes, we had a full pint. We coveted this pint of milk. For us, it was sheer liquid gold!

In the first few weeks of life, Subi nursed small amounts. Barbie's yields were high. I rationalized on the day I felt uncertain of milking that Barbie was appreciative of our services. In reality, never having children myself, I am not sure this was true. Milking her still required all hands-on deck. We bribed her with organic alpha pellets—a reward for her tolerating us and our incompetence with the task. After a week of this dual milking chore, Andrew had enough, "I am over this role. We need a milking stand."

It was becoming increasingly difficult to coordinate Barbie's schedule around Andrew's company conference calls. Andrew's Google calendar was not syncing with Barbie's farm needs.

Andrew was leaving for business trip in one day. There was no time to research yet alone build a milking stand. I would be on my own for the next three days. The bar was high. We were thoroughly enjoying our pint of goat's milk each day. "Keep those yields coming while I'm away," he said with a smile.

Initially, we had worried if we could tolerate the taste of goat's milk. Being raised in the suburbs of Minneapolis and Cleveland, we were only exposed to cow dairy. Would our pallets adjust to the flavors of goat milk? Would we be ok with the thicker texture and new smell? One week into consistent milking and we were easily converted. The creamy texture, thanks to the extra fat content of Nubian goat milk, took me back to my early childhood.

My grandfather was Italian. Much of his love was expressed through food. He trained us from a young age that mint gumdrops were vitamins. In our youth, we would dash into Grandpa's house shouting in glee, asking for our vitamins. Where other households used Flintstones daily vitamins, grandpa used herbal gum drops. Each overnight stay, he poured half and half over our morning cereal of Frosted Flakes. Growing up in the era of skim milk and with a mother who only purchased that watery concoction, half and half was a highly anticipated treat. Dairy in any form with extra fat would forever remain special in my heart thanks to my grandfather. Barbie's milk reigned supreme to me.

With Andrew away, I was feeling the pressure to continue with our pint yields. It was now early June and the sun's rays were starting to intensify. It was going to be unseasonably hot for the next few days. In this weather pattern, Barbie preferred to graze in the morning and nap in the shade of the goat barn mid-afternoon. I knew I needed to milk her during the napping hours if I were to have any success. I was on the lookout. I had witnessed the goat migration out of the pasture from the picture window in our kitchen. They walked single file, like kindergarteners going to the cafeteria for lunch. They followed the same path each and every day. There was a permanent narrow red dirt trail from the goat barn to the pastures.

I grabbed the milking tools and headed out the door to meet her at the goat barn. Once outside, the hot air caught my breath. As the sweat began to gather around my neck, I tied my hair back and mentally prepared for what lay ahead. I needed to be as calm and grounded as possible. I paused at the gate for a big inhale and exhale and then unlatched the lock and headed into her domain. Barbie heard me coming. It was clear she knew I was alone. She had the upper hand. Her eyes were wide; she was locked onto my every move. As I entered the goat barn, I saw her lying on her side in the back of the space. I could sense her plan and knew she was thinking of bolting. I had to act fast before losing her to the pasture.

I jumped once and leapt up in the air toward her. I nearly lost all the equipment in the process. Without fully understanding how it happened, I was now suddenly aware that I was on top of her. She weighed nearly as much as me and quickly tried to stand. I was draped over her neck, pushing my weight down toward the floor. I had her pinned for the time being. I placed the small feed bin of organic alpha grain in front of her. I only had a few minutes. She was a fast eater!

My brain registered that I was over her head. My hands were over her neck. Her udders were behind me. I could not milk her from this position. The only thing I knew to do was spin around and start milking quickly. In a Cirque du Soleil acrobatic like move, I flipped one hundred eighty degrees. I was now lying on my belly while my head and hands faced her teats. My legs were draped over her neck, pushing downward, trying to stay connected to the barn floor. She bellowed at the sheer awkwardness of it all. It was an accurate response to what was unfolding right before our eyes. I was covered in sweat. My hands could barely hold a grip on the glass mason jar. I was using all my might to keep her from jumping up and bolting away with me. I had flashes of my body being bounced off of her, like the children riding pigs during the pig races at the county fair.

It felt as if an hour had passed by while milking her. I had my face in the most intimate and uncomfortable spaces. I was using all of my strength to keep her pinned down. All of this was happening while she was lying on her side. Gravity was not working with us in this position. When the mason jar was about half full, I could sense I was losing the upper hand. My strength was fading. She was closer and closer to being able to stand up and dart away. The grain was gone. Sensing I was about to lose the battle, I surrendered. I sealed the half full pint-sized jar and felt grateful I had any milk at all. Once in the doorway, I turned back toward Barbie, "Please forgive me girl. And thank you for your yummy milk." I was certain we both felt assaulted. I now wondered if I needed to add goat therapy support for Barbie in my solo milking practices into our farm budget.

Day two and day three were the same. I had to sneak up on Barbie and toss my body onto hers. The image of a fish flopping out of water comes to mind. I wish we had wired the barn for a video camera. I can only imagine the amount of money these videos would have made on the television show *America's Funniest Home Videos*. After three days, she and I survived. Although my milk yields were small, I truly felt blessed to have received anything at all. I made an ultimatum with Andrew, "I will never milk her alone again without a milking stand. The past three days have been ridiculous!"

Sensing my stress and knowing he did not want to return to being my milking assistant, Andrew quickly built a milking stand. Thank goodness for DIY YouTube videos.

My new milking stand was impressive. Andrew had made a swing hinge apparatus to keep Barbie's neck in place. It had a wooden box that held the mason jar and all of the equipment. He built a wooden ramp with raised strips for non-slip action for the goats. It was the perfect height for me to sit on a small stool with her teats at the ergonomic level for my shoulders and hands. I could not believe how impressive his craftsmanship was, especially considering one of the favorite handyman memories I have of Andrew.

Our nearly one-hundred-year-old house in Asheville was having issues with the shower faucet. It was a tub/shower combination. As I strolled upstairs into the bathroom, I saw Andrew sitting on the edge of the tub with his feet resting inside. He held an array of tools fanned out as if he were holding playing cards at a poker game. His face and eyes expressed it all. Tired and confused he muttered defeatedly, "We need to call a professional." Now today, five years later, he had built an entire goat milking stand from scratch and all by himself. Wow.

The new stand functioned perfectly. Barbie and I could resume our task without a sense of shame. I enjoyed the new feeling I was experiencing. A feeling of accomplishment. A farm plan was working with a pint of milk each day. The vision I had a year before with a refrigerator filled with mason jars had come to fruition. We now had two farm success stories through the birth of Subi and the subsequent goat milk for consumption. Given the last five years on the farm, with themes focused around incompetence and massive hard work, I thoroughly enjoyed this feeling of elation. I wondered if my new-found farm success would go to my head.

I also wondered how much Samosa would have harassed me each day to drink some of the milk herself. Samosa was a foodie and would have been sitting next to me, hoping the jar would tip over for her to drink. Like the night I felt and heard her howls of glee with the birth of Subi, again I felt her presence and joy in this farm production.

15
Kameko

The winter of 2018 included snow totals above average, with colder temperatures each day too. The worst of the extreme pattern was felt in January and February. As a fair-weather farmer, I struggled with cold fingers and toes and cursed the daily demands. I stole Andrew's Carhartt coveralls and wore long underwear under my jeans. I purchased the tallest and thickest pair of wool socks I could find and pulled them up to my knees. Each bulky step I took nearly threw me off balance as I walked around the farm like the Michelin Tire Man. On top of all of this, we had hawk problems.

My chicken flock had increased to around thirty birds. Many were nearly six years old. The average age of a heritage breed is around eight. My elderly ladies were producing eggs, but the frequency had declined. The hens continued to hunt and explore the entire half acre, but one could see that their quickness and stealth-like bug hunting capabilities was comprised given their years.

Our neighbors had a few terrible run-ins with a small red tail hawk. She had killed several of their hens. We had been lucky as Samosa was quick to notice predators in the sky. This year though, we did not have Samosa. In the colder weather, we lost three Silkie hens and one rooster. The next week, the hawk killed three heritage breed birds. Although we did not witness the murders, we found the carcasses as proof. A small hawk, she had to kill the birds inside the confined space, and she was not strong enough to carry them away.

I slammed the front door as I entered the house early in the morning after finding yet another dead chicken. "She got Bloomers," I uttered under my breath and in a tone of defeat. "I am so frustrated! We have become her daily food buffet." This was her seventh catch in two weeks. At this rate, we would not have a bird left in a month. "What are we going to do?"

"You need to keep Bodhi in ChickenLand." Andrew's tone was cold.

"What are you talking about? Bodhi is not going to stay there. He will bark at the gate and go crazy if I leave him there." Andrew's solution was stated in frustration, given our farm guardian successor spent more time indoors. If a television was not involved, Bodhi spent little energy paying attention to anything on the property.

Without Samosa and without the tree foliage for coverage, in the winter the hawk was able to detect every nook and cranny of the space. She could take her time and stalk her prey. Sometimes I would find her perched on the limb of the big plum tree. In those moments, I would step through the kitchen slider door onto the deck that overlooked ChickenLand. I grabbed the obnoxious air horn Andrew purchased for me in order to scare the hawk away, and I let it rip. It worked! That is when I caught her hunting in the space. It also prompted the neighbors to text, "I hear the hawk was visiting your place again today." The air horn was loud for all involved.

My old lady hens did their best to zig and zag, seeking cover as she swooped into their domain. On certain days, you could hear the hawk screech from high in the skies above. Upon hearing her call, the chickens would frantically search for shelter. Given their elderly age, it was difficult for them to escape each day with their lives.

"Andrreeewwww!" I bellowed. "She killed Katinka and Liza Minnelli!" They were my favorite birds. They were each a fancy form of Silkie called a Sizzle. Sizzles are not a breed of chickens so much as they are words describing a showy feather. A sizzled feather curls outwardly giving the chicken a charmingly windblown appearance. Liza had been with me for five years. Katinka was her one and only offspring, and only about six months old. They looked identical though; both weighing three pounds and covered with solid black feathers. Their unusual plumage gave them the appearance of a feather boa—the inspiration for me to name her Liza Minnelli. I adored them and was heartbroken when I found them dead.

"We need a farm dog," Andrew said seriously. "Without Samosa, the whole farm is comprised."

"I don't want another animal in the house." My tone was harsh. It was an overreaction, a trigger in hearing her name and reliving the loss of her again. How could I love another like her? More importantly, how could I keep from judging the new dog? I had already set this hypothetical creature up for failure in my mind and in my heart.

"Contact the Great Pyrenees rescue organization and tell them we need an outdoor guard dog." Andrew had a perfect plan. The dog would already be trained and could live in the old space built for Keema. Four years ago, we made her a three-sided shelter should she want protection from the sun or bad weather during her days in ChickenLand. The hens now used the space to escape the rays, hanging out in the shade on hot days. The shelter could easily be converted to the perfect doghouse for our new farm guard dog. Only this time the farm protector would live one hundred percent of the time in ChickenLand.

I contacted a rescue group and as luck would have it, they had one dog that fit our needs. Typically, they preferred to receive farm dogs and rehome them inside with a family. This dog, however, had lived over four years outside with chickens and goats. We were informed he had little contact with family life and thus would be best to continue as an outdoor watchdog. He sounded like a great fit for our farm. With little information and without a meet and greet, we committed to adopting him after email correspondence. He was located in the middle of the state, about a three-hour drive.

Andrew had a solar project developing within forty-five minutes of where the rescue group operated. As he was so accustomed to doing at this point with our sixth year on the farm, he planned to pick up another animal while away on a business trip. I made an appointment for him to get the dog the following week. The rescue group asked that we meet them at the groomers. They would take the dog from the farm to be bathed and vaccinated before we adopted him. They requested we acquire him quickly, minimizing any stress given he spent zero time indoors and little in human culture. I reassured them Andrew would be there before 5 p.m.

"I'm taking the Tundra," Andrew remarked while making coffee early that morning. "The dog will have more room in the truck."

"From the one picture the farmer sent, he appears to be around the same size as Samosa. There is no need to take the truck and waste cash due to the crappy gas mileage driving across the state today. I think you should take the mini SUV, love."

"If you say so." He winked, smirked, and sauntered out the front door for a full day of travel.

Time passed slowly as I waited for Andrew to call. It was mid-January. Compared to the nasty winter weather the first of the month, today was strange as the pattern shifted. It was unusually warm, humid, and rainy. It felt more like Florida weather than home. I would have to find things to do inside today. After making three gallons of chamomile and Passionflower tea dehydrated from the summer garden and a few dozen tahini ginger molasses cookies, I turned to a book.

With growth season stunted in the winter, I had more time to enjoy quiet space. A good book was my favorite way to relax. Before I could thoroughly enjoy it though, I had to release feelings of guilt or worry in my lack of activities. It is strange how difficult it was for me to allow myself just to be. I struggled adjusting from the intense pace of summer and fall where my days were full with farm maintenance projects like weeding, mowing, mulching, power washing the barn, staining the arena fence, and the list continues. Suddenly I needed to downshift from mid-December through February, with few tasks required in the farm upkeep.

Today with the heavy rains and forced time indoors, it was easy to read. I was halfway through *The Eighty-Dollar Champion: Snowman the Horse That Inspired a Nation* by Elizabeth Letts when Andrew called. "I should have taken the truck. I can barely see out the front window as his hot dog breath is fogging it up in all of this heat and humidity. Plus, he fills the entire car. He takes up the whole hatchback!" Andrew was speaking so quickly I could barely keep up with his rambling sentences.

"What's going on?" I was beyond confused.

"What's going on is he is 135 pounds and as long as the car. He is huge! And he has clearly been with people, as he is very friendly. He keeps trying to crawl in my lap while I am driving." Andrew was laughing but feeling as bamboozled as me.

The rain continued to pour from the sky as I watched Andrew drive up the hill to our home around 9 p.m. I opened the front door and was reminded again of how confusing the weather felt. It was more like a summer July thunderstorm than anything typical of a January winter. Wearing my rain jacket and large farm muck boots, I ran out to the car. As I approached, I saw a giant white polar bear-like face staring back at me. There was not an extra square inch available in the vehicle. He was the biggest dog I had ever seen, not so much in height but in sheer mass.

"Come on, Sampson, get out of the car." We were told he was named Sampson. The rains continued and he would not budge.

"Sampson move it. You have to get out." No matter how many times we shouted his name he did not respond. Finally, with a huge tug on his collar, he stumbled out of the hatchback and made a beeline for the front door. His pace was slow but deliberate. He pushed his way through the entrance and into the living room.

Once inside, he did a full body shake, releasing moisture trapped in his fur that now splattered the foyer walls. He slowly peered around the room, pausing briefly before moseying to the area rug in front of the stone fireplace. Nothing seemed to startle him. He was completely comfortable inside the house. Andrew and I were confused. Not only was he twice the size we anticipated, he was an indoor dog. He was not the outdoor guard animal we signed up for.

The initial dog interactions went well. Yoshi jumped straight into the air toward his face and greeted him per usual. Bodhi waited for us to provide a safe space in order for them to sniff one another. None were overly enthusiastic. It was already 10 p.m. and the torrential rains continued. Farm introductions with the goats, horses, and chickens were impossible.

"Let's call it a night. I will sleep in the guest bedroom and have the new guy with me. This way I can keep a closer eye on him ... do we even know if he is potty trained?" Neither of us had an answer.

Andrew patted the new dog on the head, kissed me goodnight while wishing me luck, and went upstairs to sleep in the master bedroom with Yoshi and Bodhi. Yoshi was a needy puppy and slept in bed with us from the first night Andrew picked him up. It was a bad habit that two years later we were unable to break. Bodhi preferred to sleep on his extra-large doggie bed on the floor near my feet.

After a long day filled with anticipation and now pure confusion, I quickly drifted to sleep. I was startled awake when the new guy began snoring. The sound was deafening. The vocals ricocheted off of the vaulted ceiling in the guest bedroom. I was jolted. I could not believe how loud he was. Frustrated, I stumbled through several closets searching for a fan. I had been used to sleeping with a fan since Remmie's middle age. As a smashed faced pug, snoring was common for her but worsened over time. After several restless nights, I added white noise and finally slept. I became dependent on a fan whenever loud sounds were present from that point forward. Remmie's snoring was minimal compared to this guy. I finally found an extra fan and turned it on high—level three. It was not loud enough to muffle him.

"I am going to need an extra mug of coffee this morning. I have never heard anything like it. I can't believe it!" Andrew smiled but was unaware of what I had experienced. He poured me an extra cup and went down to the unfinished basement where his office was located when he was not on the road.

I sat at the kitchen table with my second cup of coffee. Bodhi was on the couch watching morning cartoons. Yoshi yipped at my feet, begging for me to toss his stuffed animal down the hallway for a game of fetch. In front of me was a huge solid white dog. His big brown eyes were staring back at me. I scanned him from head to toe. His hair was a mess. I noticed many patches where his pink speckled skin was visible. He looked like he had mange. His tail lacked fluff and fullness. It reminded me of an opossum tail; it was very rat like. He was a poor representation of a Great Pyrenees in this state.

Despite all of the negatives, he did have a few darling qualities. His head was very large and fluffy white. His big brown teddy bear eyes captured my heart. There was nothing but sweetness illuminating from his face, and he had massive paws, puma sized.

"What happened to you, buddy?" He gazed up and slowly sauntered toward me ramming his head between my legs. Startled for a moment, I froze. What was he doing? His behavior reminded me of a scene from the Temple Grandin movie where she engineered a holding apparatus to give her comfort. In his quick move, I, too, was now squeezing him with my legs. Perhaps providing a feeling of love and relief.

I was still surprised how comfortable he was inside the house. He navigated the floors, wandered around the furniture, and did not have an accident in the house. It was clear he had lived indoors. And, given his thin and scattered coat, we knew he would not have survived the winter weather solely outside.

I gathered all three pups and headed out on yet another rainy January day to tackle the barn chores. His pace was slow, tortoise slow. I found myself wanting to shout, "Hurry up!" more times than not. His size did not help either. He was so long; it took forever to exit through a doorway. He often stopped halfway and peered up at me. "Buddy, you're still half in the house. Move it so I can close the front door."

He heard me and then ever so slowly moved his back half outside. There appeared to be a disconnect between his head and tail and he had only one gear-low and slow.

Yoshi, Bodhi and I had the same routine. We kept the same pace and stayed near one another as I cleaned each stall, filled hay bags, filled the water buckets, and tidied the barn. The new guy was many steps behind us. He was engaged with the group and followed in all we did, yet he never caught up.

There was a pause in the rain, so I used it as an opportunity to introduce him to his new space. Bodhi, Yoshi, and I went into ChickenLand. He was yards behind us but on our route. Once through the gate, Yoshi charged after a few hens. After over a year spent with his chase energy, the birds were now comfortable around him and his pint-sized chaos. They even charged back at him a time or two. Bodhi went to the perimeter and peed on all of the trees. Finally, the new guy made it through the gate. The chickens did not mind his presence, which surprised me given how big he was. They did not bolt from him, and he was comfortable around them. He found several piles of chicken feed remnants and gobbled it all up. He strolled the entire fence line, a task that seemed to take hours.

Once he was comfortable with the boundary, I took him inside the newly formed guard doghouse. I had filled the space with several flakes of hay, perhaps too many flakes, making an almost manger-like floor for his comfort. He stayed in the shelter for a moment, sniffing each wall, and then wandered back out to search for more chicken food. There was no time like now to exit and leave him be.

He noticed as Yoshi, Bodhi, and I walked back to the barn. Without fully turning in his direction, I watched from the corner of my eye as we hustled to the house while he remained locked in his new domain. His pace quickened to catch us, although he was still very slow. He barked once in a mildly frantic tone. It was the first time I heard his vocals. He had a raspy bark. It was as if he had been a heavy smoker, smoking at least two packs a day. With his large puma paws, he pushed on the gate. I was not sure if the gate would stand up to his mass and strength as he leaned and pulled seeking his freedom. The chickens scattered with the sounds of the metal gate and chain loudly clanking against each other. I began to worry what was going to happen next.

We were quickly out of sight, and I hoped he would settle without us near. As the rain began to fall again, I went inside. From the picture window at the kitchen sink, I watched him pace, becoming more agitated. He did not seek shelter in his new home as I had hoped. "Come on buddy, go inside. You have a fluffy hay bed and protection from the elements."

I was not sure who I was talking to. Somehow, I hoped speaking the words out loud would ultimately reach him. I finally had to glance away as my heart began to break watching his stress and unhappiness.

I grabbed my iPad and busied myself in the laundry room. I selected a long video of a top instructor giving a dressage lesson to a promising student. I turned the sound up and hit play, watching while folding the clothes. Suddenly Yoshi yelped. It was his annoying, tiny-dog-high pitched bark. I could hear Bodhi's nails grind on the wood floors as he raced to the front door. I knew something was wrong. As I rounded the corner from the laundry room to our small foyer, I witnessed a giant white polar bear head peering inside through the glass panes of the front door.

"How did you escape? What are you doing up here? Did you hurt yourself?" Again, I was talking out loud, but not sure to whom. His puma paws were caked in red mud from his frantic pacing of ChickenLand. His eyes were tense. His body was stiff. He was stressed from head to toe. In the rain I grabbed the garden hose to clean his filthy feet. Once inside, I used five towels to dry his massive body. He was outside for less than thirty minutes, and I now added another load of laundry to the to-do list from this one simple task. He was so big.

Wearing my raincoat, I went back outdoors to find his breach point. Yet, I found nothing. I walked through the basement slider door to talk with Andrew in his office. "We have a problem! He will not stay in ChickenLand. He just escaped. I searched everywhere and there is not a hole in the fence or a board down. He must have jumped the gate?" I finished with a question as I had no idea how he got out.

"He has zero athleticism. I highly doubt he jumped the gate. Put him back out there." Andrew was busy with work and had little time to deal with our Houdini situation. His tone was matter of fact. The discussion was over.

Once again, I put the big guy in ChickenLand. This time I hid behind a tree. I felt like I was on a stake out. How did he escape? Like the cartoon I watched on Saturday mornings as a child, I giggled, reminiscing about Inspector Gadget. Today I was him. Only my raincoat was purple, not grey. Within a few minutes I watched as he slowly climbed the wire mesh gate. His movements mimicked a sloth. At a turtle's pace and with persistence, he painstakingly climbed his way up, over, and out. It was hilarious to watch and amazing all at once!

After drying him again, adding a second load of towels to launder today, I went to the basement to have a serious conversation with Andrew. "Ummmm I'm back. He is in the house." I laughed. Andrew glanced up from his dual computer screens, pushed his glasses to the top of his head, and hollered, "What?"

"Why is he in the house? Didn't you put him back? I do not have time for this!" He pushed his glasses back into place and began typing. I knew Andrew was stressed and busy with work. Yet, his guard dog plan was in shambles. I didn't have time to deal with this either. I did not want another dog in the house in the first place.

"He is another farm failure love. I just watched him climb the gate, sloth like. It is really funny actually. He ever so slowly climbs the wire mesh. I have no idea how he holds that big body up as he slowly creeps over the gate! He won't stay in there."

"Leave him in the laundry room. We have to wait to process this until I am done working tonight. I have a two-hour conference call that I need to prepare for right now." I knew he was cranky at the situation and not at me. After the birth of Subi and the success with milking Barbie, we assumed our farm mishaps were a thing of the past. Clearly, we needed to check our egos.

There really was nothing to talk about. He knew how to escape and without hot wiring the gates and fence line there was no way to keep him in with the chickens. I had made my mind up before Andrew finished his workday. I had surrendered to the fact that we now had three indoor dogs. They came in three different sizes from small to extra-large. I heard Andrew close his office door and knew his workday was finally over. It was 7 p.m. and we were both tired.

"Call the rescue tomorrow and return him." His tone was harsh. His words startled me.

"Return him? What are you talking about? We can't return him."

"He is not what we signed up for. Everything we were told was a lie. Just look at him. He's in terrible shape. He is very fat and has no muscle tone. He barely walks, let alone has the ability to chase after a predator and keep the farm safe. He clearly has allergies or nutritional issues, oh my goodness, look at his coat ... he doesn't have one! He is missing his bottom teeth. That's all gum that we see when his mouth is open! He has a huge pink sack hanging from under his belly. Lord only knows what that's about. Do you need me to go on? He has to go back!"

Trying to lighten the mood and tone of the room, I giggled, "That's what we can call him, False Advertisement." We both laughed. "I can't return him. I can't say those things. Although they're all true, what would happen to him? Who is going to want him? Captain Clueless is another name that works!"

"I leave for Michigan tomorrow. I think you should call the rescue and let them know what is going on here. He is not at all what they said he was." There was a sadness expressed in his words.

I knew Andrew was right. I didn't know what would become of it though. Did the farmer falsely up sell his dog? Did the rescue give us the wrong dog by mistake? Who knew the truth? I highly doubted the rescue knew what was going on. They are in the business of finding forever homes after all. There is no way they wanted to set us up for failure. It was a no-win situation.

I spent the second night in the guest bedroom. "Come on Captain Clueless. It's you and me down here again." I went to bed feeling overwhelmed and sad. It was clear from the last 24 hours that the new guy was sweet and under-loved. Any chance he had, he jammed his head between my legs, wanting to be squeezed and begging for attention and kindness. I spent the bulk of the day giving him reassurance. It did not feel like he was sad or insecure, being in a new place or following a new routine. It felt like his love tank was low. I wondered how lonely he must have been in his previous home. He seemed starved for compassion.

The next day the rain stopped. Florida weather moved out and the temperature cooled to a typical January day. I completed farm tasks as usual. He trailed behind in all I did. Bodhi and Yoshi were hot on my heels. At the end of the day, I made a large mug of golden milk. It had become my new favorite winter treat thanks to Ranjeev's influence. Ranjeev had returned to India three years ago to work in a family business, and I missed him. I felt grateful that our friendship continued despite the miles between us. I grabbed the bag of powdered turmeric he gave me during his visit last fall. I mixed it with nutmeg, ginger, and cinnamon into a mug of warm milk. Lastly, I whipped in a tablespoon of honey. It was the perfect drink to sip on while researching names on the internet.

"What are we going to call you? Captain Clueless and False Advertisement are appropriate. I do not think we should burden you with such negative names however!"

His big brown teddy bear eyes gazed into mine as his large polar bear head hung heavy in my lap. Again, he begged for love and attention.

Names like sloth and bear seemed to fit him best. I liked Oso, meaning bear in Spanish. I also liked Kuma, Japanese for bear. It was very close to Keema. Having a Keema and a Kuma on the farm made me laugh. It would be confusing. I knew Andrew and I would need several options before agreeing on a final name. Except for Bodhi, we often went through many before selecting one in our animal renaming history. The hours ticked away, my golden milk was long gone, and 1 only had two ideas for us. The search would have to continue tomorrow.

After watching him for the last two days, I realized translating the word "tortoise" would be perfect. I started a new name search. Finally, I found it. Kameko. A Japanese word meaning "tortoise child." I called Andrew immediately.

"I have three options for his name: Oso, or Kuma, which both mean bear. Or Kameko, which means tortoise child. What do you think?"

"I like Kameko. That's a cool word."

"Me too." I responded. "Kameko it is." Just as I spoke his new name, he turned and looked at me. "Do you like your new name?" He held his stare. "I think you do!"

After a month or so, he settled into a minor farm role. He wandered the driveway and sometimes explored the back of my arena. He peed on the perimeter fencing between these two points of his interest. His outdoor presence was as limited as Bodhi's. Somehow his image must have intimidated the hawk though. We did not lose a single bird the remainder of January or the month of February. He was guarding and protecting the farm on some level even though we didn't understand how.

"It's March and the leaves are popping on the trees. Perhaps this is why we haven't seen that hawk hunt the hens." Andrew was quick to point out that Kameko may have zero impact on our current farm success. Only next winter would we know if he truly negatively impacted the hawk or not.

Our challenges with Kameko presented themselves daily. He was so large that his massive presence in our small house was quite noticeable! He navigated the rooms but would barge through anything if he was on a mission. We learned not to leave glasses or mugs on tables as they were the first to tumble over while he pushed to open space. The couch and chairs were shoved into varying places as he leaned into them while lying down. Each day there were new indents in the rug to illustrate the shift.

After many weeks, he finally mastered the stairs. With his new trick through, he preferred to sleep on the landing outside our bedroom door. Even with the fan playing, his snoring would wake us. "We need to solve this. I cannot take another sleepless night." Andrew knew sleep was my preferred daily medicine. He went to the Amazon site and purchased a new gadget, checking the box for speedy delivery.

"Guess what we now own?" His pause was brief, and tone was light. "A baby gate." He shared with a laugh.

Who knew that a child free home would need a baby gate! After stumbling with the new apparatus, I finally had to mark the exact slot with a sharpie so I could accurately place the handle in the proper position to officially block the stairwell. Clearly, I was not meant to work with children's gear. I smiled in delight the first evening, knowing sleepless nights would be a thing of the past. Kameko was blocked from the upstairs and now slept against the couch on the living room rug.

Andrew returned late, around 1 a.m., after a week away. I quietly gathered the pups and allowed him to sleep while I began my day. I busied myself with outside chores, making sure all of the dogs joined me. It was early spring, and the newly planted vegetables were budding up from the ground. I picked the weeds and watered the new sprouts, eagerly awaiting their harvest in a month. After an hour or so, I returned home to find Andrew staring out the large picture window above the kitchen sink. His hair was wet from a recent shower. He looked rested but his eyes were misty.

I eased toward him, he turned and grabbed me for a big embrace. His tears released. Startled for a moment, I hugged him back, waiting for an explanation. "She came to me in a dream early this morning," he muttered. "Samosa told me to be patient with him. She sent Kameko to us and all is in order." I could feel the stress we were both holding dissipate from our bodies. We both sighed in relief. Could Samosa be at the center of this? Turning from Andrew, I looked at Kameko and wondered why Samosa would send Kameko as farm help. For now, I would let go and trust.

When friends and family inquired about the new rescue, Captain Clueless and False Advertisement were names still used in his reference. We shared tales of his incompetence and the protection he offered only inside the house and the temperature-controlled comforts of the tack room. We labeled him as a half farm failure.

Kamkeo is not even close to being the farm savvy dog Samosa was in function or personality. He does invoke a smile from me each day though. His innocence and gratitude for love and attention is captivating. He knows how to live in the moment and oozes appreciation in all we do for him. He is an excellent reminder for me, of learning how to live in a state of thankfulness at all times. My heart melts with warmth seeing him.

Through better nutrition, and grooming with therapeutic organic products, his coat is returning. I no longer see his bare skin. He now has a fluffy white tail that he wags often. He has more energy, and even trots a step or two throughout the day. He snores a little less. Still, we use the baby gate each night. In cooler weather, he walks the driveway several times a day. Each time I catch a glimpse of his large white body wandering sections of the farm it causes my heart to smile. His silhouette instills images of Samosa. I continue to have thoughts of her, especially in his presence.

16
Final Thoughts

I grew up with the books and subsequent movies *Old Yeller, Lassi,* and *Where the Red Fern Grows.* These heartwarming tales illustrate relationships between young children and their heroic dogs. The stories are timeless. The friendships between man and his best friend are full of meaning, fondness, and affection.

I adored these tales. These stories and others like it encompassed much of my childhood. Remmie was my first real understanding of the intimacy a pet owner can feel. She was often a comfort in rough times and provided deep sentiments, although, we did not have the telepathic relationship I felt the children had with their dogs of the stories I read in my youth.

Friending Samosa is where I found this relevance. I now understand the deep co-species bond where verbal communication is not necessary. Instead, the relationship is corded from the heart, not simply from the mind.

*"Not the ones speaking the same language
But the ones sharing the same feelings understand
each other."*

~Rumi

Everything in the universe moves in a rhythm and phase. The moon tells the oceans when to ebb and flow, seasons tell us when to sow and cultivate, and the darkness tells us when our day should end. As we leave one season, we enter another. Samosa represents my cycle of rebirth and soul renewal, moving me into one of my most profound life stages. She showed me how to dream a life into a reality and how to be one with all around.

I feel humans have lost the gift of full intellect experienced through Mother Nature. Life lessons are not simply taught via other people. More importantly, we learn through discovery with experiences on Mother Earth. My kinship with Samosa, and on the farm, illustrated the inevitable connections of all living things. The farm network affects my daily choices from "hearing" the bug ask for help to be lifted out of the water bucket, to not killing the grasshopper as it leaps out of my mowing path, to calling the horses into their stalls when their behavior shifts in the pasture signaling a storm is ahead. I have melted into and am learning from nature, the true state of being in proper pitch and inner tuning.

Life with Samosa taught me that every aspect of nature has something worth learning. I simply needed to pause, feel, and observe. She enforced in me how to live in the moment by stopping to smell and munch on the echinacea flowers while on our walk to collect the mail. She showed me that it's is ok and perfectly natural to pause in the task I was doing in order to witness the horses leap in joy when a cool spring breeze kicked up in the fields.

After moving to Tryon from the mountains of Asheville, snow days were minimal, so Samosa was certain to wake us up with her three low toned grunts to signal now was the time to enjoy the first snow day of the year to its fullest. She and the farm connections gave me insight into what it means to be alive. She would leap through the front door to join the horses frolicking in an inch of snow. The continued opportunities to learn from her while living within nature on our land has been one of her greatest parting gifts.

As I write this chapter, I have learned to live the last one and a half years without her physical presence. Although I have outlived her, she in a way will outlive me. Her spirit is felt on the farm and will represent our connection for an undefined amount of time. On this land I know her blood and essence live on in all of the animals she protected, in the creek waters she played in, and in the cedar tree she slept under every day. I feel her spirit in clouds knowing she guarded the skies from predators above. It is a beautiful cycle of nature and Samosa that I continue to feel with wonder.

Perfectly summarized in a song by Wiz Kalifa and Charlie Puth, the lyrics bring tears to my eyes as I sing them out loud to Samosa when I miss her most:

*"It's been a long day without you my friend
And I'll tell you all about it when I see you again
We've come a long way from where we began
Oh I'll tell you all about it when I see you again
When I see you again ... "*

To finish in humor, as all on the farm would prefer, I share Andrew's wisdom. One year ago, when I told Andrew my desire to write a book of our first six years on the farm, he smiled and declared, "I think that is a great idea. And I hope you finish the book with the sentence ...

We should have bought a condo in downtown Asheville with seven cats!"

Sneak Peak into Book Two

1

Hopi the Mustang

My eyes sensed the early dawn and I gently opened them. The room was dark, and Yoshi lay curled at my side. In the stillness, I honored that today was my forty-fourth birthday and the seventh anniversary of farm life. My holistic trainings taught me to focus on the essence of the numerology of seven. It is a positive number highlighting introspection and the attainment of wisdom. In this space, there is a celebration of continued analysis of self in relation to everything around.

I smiled thinking of the last years on the farm and honoring the seventh cycle. In this year, my teachings focused on reflection of the past in order to refine life choices for the future. It's a good year to study and analyze to prepare for more exciting years to come. Living on eighteen acres with horses, dogs, goats and chickens, and the subsequent farm failures we have endured, it is clear now in year seven that we had no choice but pay attention and learn from everything around us. As I slowly rolled out of bed to begin my day, I thought, "Oh boy, I am living a Number Seven."

Yoshi gleeful bounced alongside as I quietly crept down the stairs to the kitchen to brew coffee. Andrew was still asleep, and I certainly did not want him to feel guilty, pressure that he should be up simply because it was my birthday. While I ground the dark roast beans, Yoshi ran around the living room tossing a stuffed toy in the air. Kameko snored loudly in the background. No one was ready to begin farm chores, so I sat at the rustic kitchen table and enjoyed my warm drink. There was a strange sense of comfort this morning. I spent a little extra time staring out the window overlooking the horse pastures. Yet, I could not deny the nagging judgment that persisted in our continued ignorance of farm life. We had certainly attained wisdom in the seven years of caretaking many species of livestock. Still, nothing felt second nature in this back-to-the-land style of living.

Within an hour, Andrew was awake and normal morning rituals prevailed. The horses were grazing in the pasture while the Nubian goats frolicked at their sides. In the brisk of the fall air, the chickens ran frantically in their space, snatching up the last few bugs still alive in the season. We were living every day in Nature's world and felt gratitude being an intimate part of it.

Once inside, Andrew cooked a feast to celebrate a queen. The eggs were fresh from the morning's laying, accompanied by a locally made cinnamon toast. We still had a few pomegranates on the tree that Andrew used to garnish a beautiful bowl of yogurt and granola. In the blessed space, we stopped to reflect on my birthday and the farm's anniversary.

"We have another celebration this month my love." I looked across the table into Andrew's eyes to see if his facial movements recognized what I was referring to.

"I remember. Your crazy pony has a birthday in two weeks. Who could forget it?" We both laughed. Hopi's introduction into our lives was unusual to say the least. Here as the silly pony was about to turn ten, double digits that we celebrated as an increased wisdom and horse adulthood, we paused to reflect on our initial connection with him.

Two years ago, Andrew had played along in my search for a horse. It became an evening event where I filtered through many sales sites on the internet. After unveiling my deep childhood trauma while working with my gelding Indi, I had not been able to fully shake the raw terror. I felt guilty and conflicted as my mind was able to rationalize the event and the many positive results that grew from it and my work with Nature's View. Still, the cellular memory of the raw emotions never fully left. Subconsciously, I was more rigid and stiff than I needed to be riding Indi. It bothered me deeply. My tension felt so unfair. Indi was not the problem.

Yet, I spent many days yearning for a re-do, a fresh start to fully utilize my new equestrian skill sets. It was time to consider the offer my horse farrier stated the first day he worked on Indi. I remember his words clear as day. "Aleah, if ever you want to re-home him, please think of me." At the time, his words startled me—get rid of him? I just purchased him! Now searching through the equine ads on the internet, I focused on the option.

Less than two months after my pondering, Indi went to live on my farrier's farm. It was easy to let him go, knowing he was going to be a part of a large herd and live with two people who adored him. He would be a full-time trail horse, a role he relished. Indi's departure was a strange mix of sadness and relief. It was as if I kicked an old bad habit, releasing the past while honoring who I blossomed into because of it.

My search for a new horse intensified after Indi's farewell. Rather than reading the words of the sales ads, I fixated on the photos. One picture in particular captivated me. The horse was galloping in a field. It was not an atypical equine ad, or a unique horse photo in general. Still, his image appeared so alive and unrestricted, illuminating a wild and carefree heart. My eyes finally let go of the image to read the sales pitch. Within the description, he was labeled as "a wild mustang pony." Ah ha, now I better understood what I was feeling from the photo.

I contacted the owner and made an appointment to meet the pony. On an early Saturday morning, Andrew and I drove two hours southeast to the farm. Once on site, my heart folded. He was scrawny, underweight, and a very slight horse, even for a pony. His bone structure was delicate, and I wondered if he could support my size or if he would be better suited for a young teenager. I decided to make the most of the meeting given the distance we traveled. After pleasantries, I followed the owner and entered in the corral. The horse walked over to meet me with ease. He sniffed my hand, paused, and looked me in the eyes. Then he snorted and pranced around the pen displaying an energetic personality. I was never fearful or worried, rather a little annoyed with his cockiness. Less than an hour later, we left the farm with a promise to text a response later in the day.

As Andrew and I are accustomed to, we stopped at an Indian food restaurant in Greenville, SC to eat a buffet lunch while contemplating our decision. Mimicking our past when we processed the purchase of the farm, Yoshi as a puppy, and now the potential of this new horse, we made a list of pros and cons over a plate of paneer tikka masala, naan, and vegetarian biryani. Sipping my chai tea slowly, I stewed over the list. The nos greatly outweighed the yeses. I texted the owner a gracious, "No Thanks," finishing with best of luck regards in finding the mustang a new home.

The decision came easily, and we left the restaurant without a second thought. During the next two weeks, I forgot about him and horse shopping in general. That is until one night in August when I awoke at 4 a.m. from a very vivid dream. I couldn't sleep, my mind was in overdrive. I tossed and turned in bed over the next few hours, eager for Andrew to wake.

Finally, at 6 a.m. he said, "Why are you awake? It is so early. Simmer down."

"Oh good, you're up. You are never going to believe my dream!" I was enthusiastic and because of it, Andrew pulled himself out of bed much earlier than usual.

I paused before speaking. The dream was so real and unnerving. I needed a moment to make sure I did not sound too crazy.

"The mustang came to me. I could see his two-toned cream and black mane, small body, and grey skin tones. Like the initial photo, he was galloping in a lush grass field as he spoke, only his mouth did not move. Strangely, his words penetrated my mind. I could hear his stern voice. His tone was flat, and he told me I was wrong. That I was to partner with him. He was my horse, and I needed to pick him up right away." I was silent after reliving the dream and waited for Andrew's response.

I thought Andrew might laugh or discuss how odd the entire dream was. I thought we may rationalize the idiocy, and then we would carry on with our day. Instead Andrew smiled softly and said, "You better call her."

To my surprise, later that morning, she responded to my call. "I hoped you would change your mind." She said in an overly excited voice. "You are the only person he greeted. He's snubbed everyone else. I do have an interested buyer, but if you promise to come soon, I will sell him to you instead."

I hung up the phone and forced a smile. I felt a little uneasy even though it was my pursuit, my request. There was a deep knowing inside of me that I could not explain. Like stepping outdoors to a July mid-afternoon with an electric tingle in the air and a shift in the colors of the sky. You have an eerie sense as the heat becomes oppressive in the lack of breeze and air movement at all. In this pause, you have an inner knowing that a storm is brewing. With the same conviction, I knew driving to pick the mustang up was the beginning of something strong. I just wasn't certain what that something meant.

Acknowledgments

I humbly extend gratitude to the many who were involved in the creation of this book. From the initial spark in concept, thanks to conversations with Doug H. and Alan H. about the Fat Dog Farm failures, to encouragement and inspiration from fellow author and friends David H. and Jane R. to begin scripting the words. My heart knows no bounds in expressing my gratefulness to my life partner Andrew Makee, for having the patience and willingness with our financial support to take on such a challenge. Specially I thank my mother, Susan, who has sacrificed her time and physical body completing extra farm chores and obligations, ultimately gifting me time to finish my first book. In love of my furry best friend Samosa, who helped shape my personality and shares credit on every goal I achieve in this process.

Thanks to all my friends and family for sharing my happiness when starting the book and following with enthusiasm to completion.

A huge thank you to Chandler Bolt and Sean Sumner and all of the wonderful talented people at Self Publishing School. Without this program my book would continue to be a manuscript sitting on a desk. I appreciate the connection to my author coach, Scott Allan, who referred me to all technical players involved its production. Thank you to Emmy and Sky Rodio Nuttall, my editors, not only for catching grammatical mistakes, but also for suggesting additions that seem obvious in hindsight but would not have occurred without your services.

Finally, thank you to all of the animals who have touched my soul and opened my heart making me a better human. I honor the many places within Western North Carolina that revived my spirit and are the backdrop of my home.

Thanks Again!

Thank you for reading **Fat Dog Farm.**

If you enjoyed reading this book, please **leave a Review** on Amazon.com.

—Aleah

Made in the USA
San Bernardino, CA
21 July 2019